CHURCHES OF PORTUGAL

CHURCHES OF PORTUGAL

Text by
Professor Carlos de Azevedo

Photographs by
Chester E.V. Brummel

Scala Books, New York

This book has been done under grants from the
Graham Foundation of Advanced Studies in the
Fine Arts.

Project Directed by **Maria Teresa Train**
Design by **Stanley Stellar**
Text edited by **Fernando Batista**

Published by Scala Books, New York
Copyright © 1985

All rights reserved. No part of this book may be used
or reproduced in any manner whatsoever without written
permission. For information, address Scala Books.
1035 Fifth Ave., New York, N.Y. 10028

Distributed by Harper & Row, Publishers
ISBN 0-9357-48-66-0
Library of Congress Catalog Card Number: LC 85-050365

Production by José Brandão
Photosetting by Textype
Colour separation by Grafiseis
Printed by Printer Portuguesa
Depósito legal 5938/85

CONTENTS

THE VISIGOTHIC BEGINNING 11

THE ROMANESQUE STRENGTH 14

THE GOTHIC MAJESTY 18

THE MANUELINE EXTRAVAGANCE 25

THE RENAISSANCE ORDER 31

THE BAROQUE SPLENDOR 34

Since World War II, growing bibliography has given us a more detailed knowledge of monuments in Portugal. Apart from present day art historians we should not forget the important contribution that travellers to this country have left with their studies of portuguese art and architecture dating back as far as the 18th century. William Beckford, for example left a colourful description of life in the Monastery of Alcobaça. Published in 1795, James Murphy's book *Travels in Portugal* was the first serious approach to the study of Batalha having also proposed a solution for completing the Unfinished Chapels. Walter Crum Watson wrote a first *History of Portuguese Architecture*, published in London in 1908 and Albrecht Haupt was responsible for the first scholarly work on the Renaissance, *Die Baukunst der Renaissance in Portugal*, published in Frankfurt in 1890. However, since 1949 new fields for study and research have started, and important documentation has been published, for example, Portuguese architecture overseas from the North of Africa to India and Brazil. The efforts of Latin American scholars merit recognition, particularly those working at the University of Caracas at the Centro de Investigaciones Históricas e Estéticas. In Portugal on the other hand, the XVI International Congress of History of Art which took place in 1949 was particularly important for bringing together Portuguese and foreign art-historians. One of the pioneers of this recent generation was the late Robert C. Smith, of the University of Pennsylvania, in Philadelphia, who left a rich collection of writings, mainly on the Baroque period in Portugal and Brazil.

The aim of the present book is to provide basic information on monuments of Portugal and does not pretend to be a profound technical study. It is, rather, a survey of the most important churches in Portugal throughout the various architectural periods. Mr. Brummel's excellent photographic work is very refreshing and inaugurates this new approach to the history of architecture in Portugal.

Tomar.
Detail of window.

My interest in Portuguese architecture began with a six-week trip to Portugal in 1966. Like most first-time travellers to Portugal, I spent most of my time in and around Lisbon and was delighted to discover the unique character of much of Portuguese architecture. Subsequent trips to Portugal, in particular a five-month stay in 1981 funded by a generous grant from the Graham Foundation of Chicago, enabled me to discover more and more of the diversity and richness of ecclesiastical architecture in Portugal. My goal as an art-historian and photographer is simple: to show people the uniqueness of Portuguese architecture and to motivate people to discover for themselves a relatively unknown area of Western European architecture. This book is intended primarily as a first step in a continuing study of the churches of Portugal.

All books are collaborative efforts and I would like to take this opportunity to thank all the people who have advised and encouraged me in this project:

Marty Forscher, Vic Gorecki, Bruno Hauser, Michael Maddox, Bob Meyer, Mickey Pallas, Dave Phillips, Rebecca Pope, Selwyn Schwartz, Howard Silver, Patt Snyder and Don Tomer. Special thanks to Linda Casey and Nancy Rosen, Berkey Marketing Corporation; William Giordano of Nikon, Incorporated; Nicholas Sapieha; Henry Tabor and Nicholas Callaway.

Among the scholars who have generously shared their knowledge with me are Professors Edson Armi of the University of North Carolina at Chapel Hill; Pramod Chandra, Harvard University; George Kubler, Yale University; Robert Loescher of the School of the Art Institute of Chicago; Alex Mitchell, Lake Forest College; Earl Rosenthal, The University of Chicago; Franz Schultze, Lake Forest College; the late Robert C. Smith, the University of Pennsylvania; Fr. Harrie Vanderstappen, University of Chicago and Hellmut Wohl, Boston University. I would like to thank them for their advice and their example. I would also like to thank Carter H. Manny and the Graham Foundation Chicago for all their support and Carlos de Azevedo, a man I feel honoured to call «colleague».

In Portugal my work was grately enhanced by the assistance of Alberto Marques, José Carrasco, Nuno Almeida and Luís da Ponte of the Portuguese National Tourist Office. I also extend most grateful appreciation to Rita Sales, Maria do Carmo Pina, Maria Alice Faria and João Pedro Palma-Ferreira of the Ministério da Cultura in Lisbon for all their help.

One day in 1981, as I was photographing the tomb of Inês de Castro at Alcobaça, the light was getting dim. I was rubbing my eyes and one of the guards told me he had observed that I was working very hard. In my poor Portuguese I told him that yes, I was working hard, but that I was engaged in a «trabalho do coração», a «work of the heart». I told him how much I wanted to share with people the beauty of Portuguese art and how much difficulty I was having in finding someone willing to publish my work. He told me to remember an old Portuguese proverb: «há-de ser o que Deus quiser», which, very loosely translated means «Whatever happens will happen because God wills it». With that in mind I would like to voice my deepest thanks to the people of Portugal, especially José Cabral, Filipe de Sousa and Jack, Clara and Miguel Glatzer for sharing with me their love of all things Portuguese and to Maria Teresa Train of Scala Books for helping make this dream of mine come true.

Most of all I would like to thank my mother and my late father without whose love and understanding this project would never have been finished. It is to them I most lovingly dedicate all my work. We finally did it. N. S.

Batalha.
Flying buttresses.

THE VISIGOTHIC BEGINNING

THE Romans, attempting to bind their military conquests under a superior civilizing force, set out to «romanize» vast areas of western Europe Primarily through the imposition of their language and institutions, they succeeded in strengthening their empire. As a result of these efforts, Roman culture spread and flourished throughout Rome's dominions, reaching its westernmost province, Lusitania — which corresponds roughly with present-day Portugal — by 27 B. C. However, this remarkable process of cultural integration and regeneration was abruptly halted in the fifth century, when the Asiatic Huns surged into eastern Europe, impelling previously settled Germanic tribes — Goths, Vandals, Swabians — to pour through the borders of the empire in a series of devastating migratory waves that culminated in the fall of Rome in 476 A. D. The subsequent withdrawal of Roman protection and influence from romanized Europe led to a chaos that became known as the Dark Ages, during which local civilization declined to its lowest point.

Eventually, Roman influence was replaced by that of Christianity, and the emerging monastic orders became the major civilizing force. Through them, the Church assumed its vital role in community life. The rural Christian society emerging from the Dark Ages looked upon the Church as the only source of culture and learning, for the clergy became the guardians of the Latin language and they dominated education throughout the Middle Ages. The Visigoths — a subdivision of the Goths, who had settled in the Roman provinces of Hispania and Lusitania after the collapse of the empire — converted to Christianity in the early seventh century and founded a unified Christian Kingdom that covered the entire Iberian peninsula. They admired the classical civilization of the Romans, whose extensive ruins littered their land, and, on the basis of this, strove to develop a culture of their own. Much of the surviving art from this period is consequently Roman in character. Indigenous and other sources of inspiration are discernible, however, particularly in the architecture. Visigothic churches, for example, displayed horseshoe arches long before the arrival of the Moors and Oriental art. This arch is the most interesting feature of the Visigoth's architecture, for they used it as both a structural and a decorative element whereas the Romans had used it only decoratively. However, it remains uncertain whether the Visigothic type of arch originated from a local Iberian tradition or was imported from Persia in ancient times. It may also have been introduced by the Visigoths themselves in the sixth century, though — given the absence of this feature in the architecture of other, related, Germanic peoples — this seems less likely. Elsewhere in Europe similar signs of independence from Roman ideas also began to appear. The theory that ancient Rome and Byzantium were the only inspiration for preromanesque European architecture holds true only for Italy; in countries more distant from Rome, an equally strong inspiration came from indigenous sources. Like the Visigothic churches of Iberia, the timber constructions of Scandinavia and Britain and the stone churches of the Balkans exemplify this tendency. Visigothic art is therefore an amalgam of Roman, Germanic, Christian, and indigenous sources. However, we can already perceive in this the origins of a synthesis which, after long gestation, was to culminate in the romanesque.

The earliest churches built on Iberian soil were Visigothic. In 711, however, the Moors conquered the Visigoths and subsequently overran the entire peninsula. Their influence gave birth to a unique style — part Christian, part Arabic — that was reflected in alterations to many of the earlier buildings. The Moors, who brought with them an advanced culture and religion (Islam), were nonetheless tolerant of local customs and allowed the Christians to retain their churches and worship in them. Therefore the Christians living under Islamic rule, known as Mozarabs, were able to hold on to their old Visigothic traditions, though their art, especially in its decorative elements, was influenced by Islamic taste. Thus the Mozarabic churches retained the Visigothic horseshoe arch and basilican plan, although their arches sometimes reflect the Arabic preference for greater height. In other respects Mozarabic architecture is far different from that of the Moors, remaining faithful to the early Christian model. Though few preromanesque churches have survived, some still stand in Portugal. Of these, some are in ruins while others remain, stone sentinels of a bygone age, unwilling to reveal the mystery that seems to enshroud them. These rare churches, the infant buildings of Christianity, represent the first uncertain step in a long architectural tradition.

Two churches typify this early period, São Pedro de Balsemão and Santo Amaro de Beja. The latter located outside the city walls of Beja in southern Portugal, is built on the basilican plan. Its interior is divided into a nave and two aisles by short arcaded columns with unusual capitals, probably Visigothic or Mozarabic. The nave ends in a simple chancel flanked by two small chapels, one at the head of each aisle. Santo Amaro may date back as far as the seventh century, though the building seems to have been substantially altered in later periods.

The church of Lourosa was begun, according to an inscription over its entrance, in 912 A. D. Built after the Moorish invasion, Lourosa — a three-aisled basilica with two arcades of horseshoe arches dividing the interior in the Visigothic manner — is considered Mozarabic structure. As in Santo Amaro, the chancel stands between two small chapels, though here these open onto a transept. The central nave is longer than the lateral aisles and the transept has relatively short arms. Particularly noteworthy is the high twin-arched window set just under the roof line of the east wall, which typifies Mozarabic and Moorish fenestration. This window type, the *ajimez*, is characteristically made up of an arch which, when split by a central supporting pillar, yields two smaller arches of identical size. The church of Lourosa is a building of somber architecture, almost devoid of decoration. Interestingly, nearly all the material employed in its construction was taken from earlier Roman and Visigothic buildings, hence its special archeological significance.

The most interesting preromanesque temple in Portugal, however, is the funerary chapel of São Frutuoso de Montélios, outside the city of Braga, in the north. This small building, topped with a central dome, was first built in the seventh century to house the tomb of Saint Frutuoso; subsequently destroyed by the Moors, it was rebuilt in the eleventh century. Its plan, based on the Greek cross, comprises four rectangular arms, one of which contains the doorway. The other three end, on the inside, in arching walls. Although the church's interior is Visigothic, it has a stangely Byzantine appearance. Four large horseshoe arches mark the central crossing they rest on a broad frieze that runs across all the inside walls. Each of the four horseshoe arches encloses three smaller ones supported by slender columns with Corinthian capitals. Although the horseshoe arches and the stylized floral design of the frieze and the capitals are typically Visigothic, the overall arrangement is distinctly Byzantine. Its resemblance to the fifth-century mausoleum of Galla Placidia in Ravenna, is particularly striking; the plan, the spatial arrangement, and even the technique used to support the dome are similar in both. On the exterior, there are other affinities too, like the shallow arcading on the walls which in the ravenate model is always a round-headed arch, whereas in São Frutuoso it alternates with a pointed design. The presence of Byzantine influence on Iberia, limited though it was, can be traced back to the arrival of Byzantine travellers in the sixth century. Why this influence made itself felt in the building of São Frutuoso and not elsewhere, remains a mystery.

THE ROMANESQUE STRENGTH

In the eighth century, less than three hundred years after the Roman Empire's dismemberment by northern tribes, Europe faced a new and powerful threat from the south: that of Islam. From their base in North Africa, the Moors stormed over the Strait of Gibraltar in 711 and moved rapidly across Iberia, occupying the whole peninsula except for a small area in the northwest. Although they failed to gain a foothold in France, they retained influence in Spain until 1492 when their last Spanish enclave fell. Portugal's emergence as a nation occurred during this turbulent era.

The mountainous Christian stronghold that had withstood the foreign invasion, gradually forcing the Muslims to retreat southward, eventually grew into the Spanish kingdom of León. In 1087, Alfonso VI, king of León, launched a massive military campaign against the Moors and asked for help from a number of French knights who were known for their fighting skills. Two of these foreign guests, Count Henry of Burgundy and his cousin Raymond, so impressed the king that he, to reward them, offered them his only two daughters in marriage. Raymond thus married Urraca, heiress to the Spanish throne, while Henry took her sister, Teresa, whose dowry included a county called Portucale. The two couples did not, however, live happily ever after. As soon as king Alfonso died, a bitter family quarrel erupted; as a result the county of Portucale broke free of the kingdom to become a satellite of Burgundy, Henry's native land, and in 1139 Henry's son, Afonso Henriques, was proclaimed first king of Portugal. His successors subsequently conquered all the Moorish-held lands south of their small kingdom, until they put together the roughly rectangular nation we know as Portugal. It is now one of the oldest nations in Europe, since it has preserved its borders virtually unchanged since it was reconquered in the thirteenth century.

At the time of Portugal's birth, intense building activity was sweeping across Europe. Churches and monasteries were rising everywhere and pilgrimage roads, linking one religious center with another, were making communication once again possible. The imposition of papal authority and the civilizing work of monastic orders had achieved a spiritual unity that transcended national differences. A new architectural style, the romanesque, emerged from this religious reawakening; as an expression of the new spiritual unity, it soon gained acceptance throughout western Europe.

In Portugal as in Spain, the romanesque period coincided with the most critical phase of the reconquest, the struggle to oust the Muslims, a period of great violence and insecurity. The architecture of its castles, walled cities, and churches therefore reflected a need for both physical protection and spiritual refuge. The new style, with its thick walls and strong features, satisfied the notion of the Church as bastion against Islam; but it was imposed upon the Visigothic tradition only slowly, because of the civil strife and the relative isolation of the Iberian peninsula. However, because of its rulers' Burgundian origins, Portugal was eventually brought under French influence. The architects of the time were generally members of the monastic orders, which along with the great pilgrimages, carried the new style into Portugal shortly after it became independent from Spain. As already mentioned, monks were the custodians of literacy, serving as both scholars and teachers. Therefore Afonso Henriques, Portugal's first monarch, invited the Benedictines of Cluny to lay the foundations of learning in his new kingdom. This initiative succeeded so well that, within few years, over one hundred monasteries were built in the region already reconquered from the Moors. The Cluniac order like the monarchy, had its roots in Burgundy; therefore it played a paramount role in imposing French influence on romanesque architecture as it developed in Portugal. The most important pilgrimage center in Europe during the Middle Ages, on the other hand, was the town of Santiago de Compostela in northwestern Spain, near Portugal's northern border. Pilgrims from all over Europe travelled the road from France to Santiago in order to see the relics of St. James, and part of their knowledge was carried southward. In addition, wandering craftsmen in search of work sometimes travelled this busy route and ventured to the farthest bounds of the reconquered territories; this explains the presence of French artisans as far south as in Lisbon by the mid-twelfth century.

Although French influence in Portugal was indeed strong, the native adaptation of the romanesque style often showed uniquely Iberian characteristics. Given the warlike conditions of the time, for instance, many Portuguese cathedrals incorporated defensive features such as battlements. Strength and austerity are therefore most characteristic of the native style. Romanesque architecture in Portugal, as elsewhere in Europe, is best expressed in its churches. These arose in the path of the reconquest, which, ran southward from Braga to Coimbra, Lisbon and Évora. All the important cities along this path were graced by fine romanesque cathedrals that served as visible symbols of the new status quo. Because of the immense difficulties of transport and the limited technical knowledge of the time, these vast structures were built at great human and financial cost. Their construction was therefore slow; sometimes they grew through many decades, finally being completed in the early Gothic period or even later. Subsequent alterations and additions have further complicated the stylistic composition of most. Consequently, none can be said to be entirely romanesque. The fortresslike appearance of these first cathedrals, however, reflects Portugal's struggle to consolidate her budding independence.

Probably the best example of a romanesque cathedral in Portugal is the Old

Cathedral, or Sé Velha, in Coimbra. Designed by French masters Robert and Bernard, it was built between 1160 and 1180, when Coimbra was the expanding kingdom's capital. This cathedral has a solid, fortified exterior, with a line of battlements running across the whole building. The plan is based on the Latin cross; typically, a square tower with cupola covers the crossing. The west façade is austere and impressive in its stalwart simplicity, with a finely carved portico surmounted by a matching window opening, deeply recessed. The east end, where the chancel is flanked by two semicircular chapels, is triapsidal. The three-aisled interior is very romanesque; it has the austere grandeur characteristic of the period. The high nave divided into arcade and triforium, has a barrel vault supported by transverse arches carried on piers; the lateral aisles are cross-vaulted. The nave's arcade is round-headed, a standard feature of the period, and the triforium above it has a wide ambulatory supported over the full width of the aisle vaults. The eye, however, is inevitably led toward the chancel, which is dominated by a beautiful Flemish altarpiece in gilt wood executed between 1498 and 1508. Major additions to the original romanesque building included the adjoining cloister, in the Gothic style, as well as the magnificent north portal, thought to be one of the first signs of the Renaissance in Portugal.

The cathedral in Lisbon was commissioned by king Afonso Henriques immediatley after the Christian reconquest of that city; construction began in 1160 on the site of the old mosque. This is again a building of solid, massive architecture. As in Coimbra, the design is the work of masters Robert and Bernard, which explains the similarities between the two cathedrals. The façade here is more typically romanesque, however, as it includes two powerful side towers and a rose window over the portal. Unfortunately, the building was badly damaged during the earthquake of 1755; at that time, the chancel collapsed. It was rebuilt in the eighteenth century, with a manificent baroque organ on each side (one of these has now been removed to Santa Engrácia). The Gothic ambulatory with its side chapels was spared by the earthquake and the whole building was restored to its former state in the twentieth century.

The cathedrals in Lamego, Oporto, and Braga, which were initially built in the romanesque style, have suffered so many restorations that they are no longer truly characteristic of the period. In Braga, for instance, the introduction of the eighteenth-century choir and organs has significantly broken the austere harmony of the romanesque interior. By contrast the cathedral of Évora, erected in the twelfth and thirteenth centuries, has a romanesque plan, but the structure and decorations are already Gothic in style. Again there are two towers at the front, some romanesque windows, battlements, and a deeply recessed portal. In the interior there is an elegant nave covered by a vault that rests on a broken-arch framework. The vaulting, the rose windows of the transept, the cupola, and, finally, even the cloister and the general proportions of the great church are all already Gothic. Évora, therefore, is typical of the transition from romanesque to the latter style. However, the chancel was completely rebuilt between 1721 and 1746 on the basis of designs by Ludovice, John V's architect. But the most characteristic feature of Évora cathedral is the conical structure built over the dome, which establishes the clear influence of romanesque churches in Poitou (France).

Apart from the cathedrals, Portugal contributed to romanesque with many smaller churches adopting simple, rectangular plans. In the north, these were made of stone blocks, with wooden roofs. In the south, masonry was used for the walls and vaults were reserved mainly for the chancel. The capitals and portals of these churches sometimes display remarkable sculpture. Many beautiful stone churches still dot the lush green hills of northern Portugal. The twelfth-century church of São Salvador, in Travanca, is a typical example. Built as part of an old Benedictine monastery, it has a handsome sculptured portico and an impressive, battlemented side tower. The use of such defensive towers, intended to provide refuge in the event of Moorish or Spanish raids, again reflects the warfare and instability of the time. A similar tower can still be seen beside the church of Manhente, near Barcelos. Here, as in Travanca, the tower is detached from the church.

The church of Bravães, not very far from Braga, boasts on its west façade the most ornate romanesque portal in Portugal. The jambs and archivolts of this magnificent doorway are covered with a series of iconographic reliefs displaying a variety of animal, bird, and human subjects; the tympanum, which is here supported by two stylized bull heads, depicts Christ in majesty flanked by two human figures. Apart from the main portal, the interior contains an interesting frieze of Moorish-influenced design, and the south portal also bears a fine tympanum with a bas relief representing the holy lamb. Although romanesque sculpture obviously tells the story of the Bible and was believed to give protection against evil spirits, its mythological language has not been fully deciphered. The bull, for example, is generally thought to represent the death of Christ, but the origins of this and other hidden meanings probably lie in more ancient pagan cults. Equally interesting portals exist in the churches of Tabuaço, Ferreira de Aves, Melgaço, and Roriz.

The most unusual romanesque building in Portugal, however, stands within the famous Convent of Christ, which crowns the riverside town of Tomar in central Portugal. Founded by the order of the Knights Templars in 1160, this fortress-convent was not completed until the seventeenth century. Therefore its vast complex developed in several architectural styles around the original twelfth-century sanctuary of the Templars: a beautiful rotunda, or *charola*, modelled after the Holy Sepulcher in Jerusalem. The centralized plan of this sanctuary, once used by the knights as their private chapel, reflects the Oriental influence to which the order had been exposed in the Holy Land. Within this structure, eight pillars support a two-story octagonal drum covered by a cupola; an ambulatory encircles this octagon and separates it from the polygonal exterior wall. In the sixteenth century an elegant Manueline nave was attached to the rotunda without impairing the beautiful octagon, which now functions as chancel of the church. The exterior reflects the design of the centralized structure; this still uses an early type of buttress rising from ground level to the roof line, where sixteenth century battlements crown the parapet. An illuminated page in a book dating from 1506 shows that the *charola* and the adjoining bell tower were also crowned by small pyramids. Unfortunately these have disappeared. Meanwhile, the Order of the Temple was dissolved by Pope Clement V and a new Order — the Order of Christ — was created by King Dinis, and the great complex at Tomar eventually became their seat.

THE GOTHIC MAJESTY

In the mid-twelfth century, when Portugal's first great cathedrals were still in the planning stage, experienced builders in northwestern France had begun to experiment with an old architectural feature: the pointed arch. Although this type of arch had been known since ancient times and was widely employed in Oriental architecture, its use had previously been merely decorative. Now, however, with the surge of Christianity and the increasing complexity of religious architecture, there was a new need for structural innovation. The rounded arch, which had been used in both Roman and romanesque structures, posed great problems in vaulting a church, mainly because the aisles were generally shorter and lower than the nave; the pointed arch, by contrast, was now found to offer a more flexible system that could accomodate varying spans and roof levels. The revolutionary discovery made possible the widening of the stone vaulting system, which, when supported by adequate wall abutments, also satisfied the need for more capacious interiors. It was further discovered that walls no longer had to be so thick, since the system's great stresses fell on the arches themselves, the pillars, and the buttresses. As a result, more space for window openings could be allowed. This architectural combination of pointed arches, rib vaulting, and improved buttressing led to the evolution of less weighty structures and a new style of ever-increasing of verticality and airiness. Eventually, these structures were to become our symbols of medieval spirituality.

The Gothic movement, as this current of new ideas came to be known, was slow to mature, however, and some European countries clung to old forms well into the thirteenth century. The transition from the romanesque to Gothic advanced at different speeds in different areas. Italy, for example, was slow to adapt, whereas northern France and England adapted quickly. The transition in Spain and Germany, on the other hand, was accelerated by the importation of fully developed Gothic from France. As had happened with the romanesque style, the gradual acceptance of Gothic forms was due largely to the ever-growing influence of the monastic orders, and it was the Cistercian monks of Burgundy who first adapted the pointed arch to the traditional transept crossing of naves.

The Cistercians, a branch of the Benedictines, were established in reaction to increasingly ostentatious displays of wealth and power on the part of the infuential Benedictine order of Cluny. At a time when monarchs considered themselves vicars of God, the Benedictines of Cluny had come to wield great influence in the affairs of state; their monasteries flaunted this in a variety of ways, as in the richness of their architecture. The Cistercians, on the other hand, now sought to restore monasticism to its former austerity and detachment from the outside world; their establishments were to be entirely self-sufficient and governed by a strict code of conduct comprising poverty, silence, and manual labour. Their doctrine spread rapidly from Burgundy to other parts of Europe, and in 1138, like the monks of Cluny before them, the Cistercians, at the invitation of the nation's first king, entered Portugal.

Once in Portugal, the Cistercians contributed greatly to the reoccupation and agricultural development of the lands recovered from the Moors; therefore the king chose them to establish a model community in the reconquered regions north of Lisbon; it was destined to become Portugal's most important monastery. In 1178, as their rules prescribed, the monks began building on a lonely site, around which the present town of Alcobaça subsequently developed.

The abbey church of Our Lady of Alcobaça is the largest church in Portugal; it is perhaps also the grandest of all Cistercian buildings in Europe and the one whose structure best reflects the emerging Gothic style. Although the exterior of the abbey suffered substantial alterations in the seventeenth and eighteenth centuries, its ornate baroque façade presents an interesting contrast with the interior. The long and impressive white stone nave, devoid of later ornamentation, retains its uplifting spaciousness. It has a noble beauty, at once cold and grandiose, that freely combines the Cistercian severity with newer ideas.

The ribbed vaulting is braced by a succession of large, pointed, transverse arches on lofty piers; the vaulting shafts of these piers are noteworthy in that they do not descend to the ground but are supported on corbels, whereby the architect has considerably widened the capacity of the nave. Because nave and aisles are of uniform height and vault design, the windows are set high in the aisle walls; their light reflected on the white stone has been likened, in poetry, to moonlight. The east end is apsidal, with an ambulatory and round columns set beneath tall, narrow windows.

Although Cistercian norms originally forbade all forms of sculptural adornment, the transept in Alcobaça now contains the magnificent fourteenth-century tombs of King Pedro I and Inês de Castro, two ill-fated lovers whose, gruesome story has fired the imagination of writers since the Middle Ages. In brief, crown prince Pedro, a young widower, is said to have secretely married Inês de Castro, his former wife's lady-in-waiting, who was also his long-time lover. But Inês, a Spanish beauty, belonged to a noble and ambitious family; therefore Pedro's royal father and his court, on discovering the deed, arranged to have her murdered. When, shortly after, Pedro ascended the throne, he took his revenge: he publicly crowned the body of his murdered lover and forced every courtier in the kingdom to kiss her decomposed hand. This macabre coronation is said to have taken place in the abbey church of Alcobaça. The richly carved tombs, among the finest examples of funerary sculpture in Europe, are so positioned that the lovers may awaken to face each other on Judgment Day; a remarkable relief depicting that day adorns the lower left side of Inês de Castro's tomb. The sarcophagi are surmounted by recumbent statues of the deceased, both with peaceful expressions.

Because the monastery of Alcobaça was modelled after the Burgundian abbey of Clairvaux, the disposition of its buildings around a central cloister follows the pattern established by earlier Benedictine monasteries, whose religious and agricultural needs where the same. The church nave therefore opens into the south gallery of the cloister, whereas the remaining buildings are arranged in accordance with their specific functions: those reserved for the monks were built as a continuation of the transept and chancel of the church on one side of the cloister; those for the lay brothers, recruited to do the heavier work on the fields, are on the opposite side. Consequently the chapter house, which served as a ceremonial meeting room, stands alongside the church transept and opens into the cloister through wide twin bays, from which lay brothers, who were allowed only in the nave, could watch the proceedings inside. The room itself has groined vaulting that springs from central pillars. The abbey's kitchen, on the north gallery, is truly remarkable. It has huge marble tables and hooded chimneys some forty feet high, surmounting vast ovens in which it was possible to roast six oxen at once. Through the center of this runs an underground stream, where the monks not only rinsed their dishes but also fished for trout and eels for the Friday observances. A service hatch communicates between the kitchen and the refectory, or dining hall; opposite this is an elegant lavabo at which the monks washed their hands before and after meals. The fourteenth-century Cloister of Silence, whose vaulted galleries link all the buildings, served as a model for the Gothic cloisters adjoining the cathedrals in Coimbra, Lisbon, and Évora. The ground floor has arcade openings with paired columns supporting arches topped by a rose window; the second story is a simpler sixteenth-century addition. Finally, the King's Hall, opening into the church nave, is a handsome addition dating from the eighteenth century. It contains a collection of statues of Portuguese monarchs carved by the monks themselves some time after the order's ban on sculpture had been relaxed.

Although the monastery of Alcobaça played a significant role in the introduction of new ideas, it is not truly characteristic of the transition in Portugal. The cathedral of Évora, farther south, is a more representative example of the slow fusion of old and new forms that typified the period. As mentioned in the previous chapter, this building, which stands on a height overlooking Évora, was erected in the twelfth and thirteenth centuries. Though it displays a variety of architectural styles and adornments, structurally it remains a combination of late romanesque and early Gothic design. The stark, fortified exterior continues in the romanesque tradition; the main façade is flanked by sturdy twin towers and has a deeply recessed doorway with beautiful statues of the apostles set into the jambs. The imposing interior, built of large blocks of warm-coloured stone, has a tall nave resting on a broken arch framework. The nave has an elegant triforium, inspired by the one in Lisbon's cathedral, but no clerestory; whereas the scheme is typically romanesque, the predominant use of the pointed arch and the sheer verticality of the whole design are clearly Gothic in character. The transept arms are lit by two large Gothic rose windows, and the chancel, as we have pointed out, is an eighteenth-century reconstruction faced with coloured Italian and Portuguese marble. Finally when, in the sixteenth century, Évora gained prominence as a prosperous cultural center, the cathedral acquired many treasures, such as paintings and objects of silver, that are now displayed in the cathedral chapels and the treasury; the richly carved choir stalls and impressive organ also date from this time (1562). Throughout the thirteenth century the Gothic style matured in northern France. The flying buttress, which had been designed to transmit rather than resist the outward and downward thrust of the vault, now made possible the construction of churches that were mere shells of ribs and piers. Windows and doorways consequently grew in size and complexity, piers soared to new heights, and interior spaces became richly endowed with light and shadow. In Portugal, however, although Gothic techniques were already being employed at this time, the ideal of beauty rested upon the romanesque well into the fourteenth century. The reason for this slow acceptance of the Gothic style lies both in the military spirit of the struggling kingdom, which placed great value on the solidity of its architecture, and in the nation's sunny climate, which made window space less of a priority. Nevertheless, the tide of architectural taste began to turn after 1249, when the expulsion of the Moors from their last foothold in southern Portugal marked the beginning of a new era in the nation's history: Portugal's uncertain borders were hereafter to remain firmly established under the banner of Christianity. The conclusion of the long struggle to oust the Moors brought a certain feeling of fulfilment to the young kingdom, and, very gradually, the previously unrivalled predominance of the fortress-church began to decline. Although Gothic churches in Portugal would, until the fourteenth century, incorporate features of the new style into work that was primarily romanesque in spirit, this change in mood served to pave the way from martial austerity to the fifteenth century's sudden shift toward Manueline extravagance. Halfway through the thirteenth century, therefore, while romanesque churches were still rising in Portugal, others were already making systematic use of the pointed arch. An early example is the church of Santa Clara, in Santarém, whose simple features are repeated in many later churches throughout the country: a high central nave balanced by aisles, large pointed arches, and a polygonal apse. The convent church of Santa Clara-a-Velha, in Coimbra, is a more interesting example dating from the early fourteenth century. Like the abbey church in Alcobaça, this is a «hall church», characterized by nave and aisles of equal height. The nave here has a pointed barrel vault, however, while the aisles are rib-vaulted. Interestingly, despite the use it makes of typically Gothic features such as lancet windows, there remains a certain heaviness to the walls which is reminiscent of the romanesque style. The fourteenth-century fortress-church of Leça do Bailio, near Oporto, also reflects the romanesque tradition. Although it employs the pointed arch as well as Gothic windows, it has a heavily fortified exterior and a massive side tower typical of earlier times.

In Portugal the late Gothic style did not completely impose itself upon the deeply rooted romanesque until the end of the fourteenth century; it took an event of enormous historical significance to inspire the building which was to seal this final phase of the transition. This came when, in 1383, Portugal's founding dynasty died out without leaving an heir. The vacant throne was hence contested by the king of Castile and John, grand master of the order of Avis, who was also the illegitimate son of Pedro I and Teresa Lourenço. Portugal's very existence was at stake here, for if John were defeated the country would pass under Spanish rule. The Castilian and Portuguese armies finally met on August 4, 1385, at Aljubarrota, near Alcobaça; before the decisive battle, however, John had vowed to raise a magnificent abbey in honour of the Holy Virgin if she granted him victory.

Today, the monastery of Our Lady of Victory rises triumphantly near the field where the battle was fought, hence the name by which it has become known: Batalha. By inspiration, Batalha is therefore a masterwork of Portuguese Gothic architecture risen in remembrance of Our Lady's intervention in that fateful battle. In terms of design, however, it has been seen as a deliberate attempt to shape a national style from a variety of foreign sources. The result is eclectic yet essentially Portuguese; it is above all else, the final triumph of Gothic taste in Portugal. The superb limestone church bristles with an array of pinnacles, gables, flying buttresses, and, where previous buildings bore battlements, lacelike balustrades of carved tracery. Despite this profusion of Gothic embellishments, the striking flatness of the roofs makes the building look typically Portuguese. The exterior is replete with vertical lines, although the proportions of certain features, the long walls and the structure of the Founder's chapel seem to destroy this verticality. The west front also suggests the influence of the English perpendicular style. This last analogy gains weight when one considers that the founder's wife was Phillipa of Lancaster, daughter of John of Gaunt, and that English archers had helped her husband defeat the Castilians, thereby sealing a long alliance between Portugal and England. English influence seems especially evident in Batalha's richly decorated west façade, whose main surfaces are divided into tiers of decorative panels typical of the perpendicular style. This façade has a very fine sculptured portico topped by a large window in Flamboyant Gothic design, but, as Dominican norms prescribed, it incorporates no bell towers.

The monastery's construction continued throughout the fifteenth century, so that pure Gothic features are now mingled with hints of the Manueline. Begun by the Portuguese architect Afonso Domingues in about 1388, most of the church and part of the Royal Cloister were completed by a certain master Huguet of unknown nationality between 1402 and 1438. The church itself is cruciform, with an apsidal east end and tall lancet windows. The soaring interior of the nave has clustered piers rising to small foliated capitals and quadripartite vaults; the latter have a third rib, again suggesting the possibility of English influence. Unlike Évora, the nave here has a clerestory but no triforium; it is stark and lacking in ostentation. In contrast, the adjoining Founder's Chapel is richly decorated in the late Gothic style. This chapel has a magnificent star vault carried on an octagonal drum pierced by eight lancet windows. Pointed arches link the piers supporting the lantern, and large, flamboyant stained glass windows light the interior. As its name implies, the chapel contains the tombs of John I and his English queen, set under carved Gothic canopies. Their children, also entombed here, include the planner of Portugal's famed voyages of discovery, Prince Henry the Navigator.

The Royal Cloister, on the north side of the church, leads into the chapter house, which has a single vault of rare audacity. Here, the architect succeeded, after two unsuccessful attempts, in vaulting the wide room without using intermediate supports; this engineering feat involved such danger, however, that the work itself was assigned to convicts under sentence of death. Ironically, the fateful vault now shelters Portugal's Tomb of the Unknown Soldier. The Royal Cloister, on the other hand, reflects the influence of Alcobaça and has a beautiful lavabo in one corner. Master Huguet is also responsible for having begun the octagonal pantheon behind the church apse, but his sudden death in 1438 left the chapels unfinished. After this date, master Fernão d'Évora built a second cloister, more sober than the first, under the royal patronage of king Afonso V, whose blazon decorates the vaulting keystones in the galleries.

The final period of work in Batalha coincided with the heyday of the Manueline style and therefore marks the origin of much of the florid decoration that runs through the monastery. Directed by master Mateus Fernandes, this decorative work culminated in the Royal Cloister, where the Gothic arcade openings were filled in with an intricate tracery of carved marble resting on small, slender columns, themselves decorated with carved shells, pearls, and twisted cords. The result is a hybrid of spectacular beauty. At the same time, the doorway leading into the Unfinished Chapels was richly ornamented with equally exuberant Manueline carvings, although in the end the pantheon itself was left unroofed.

As was to be expected, Batalha was strongly influential in the shaping of contemporary buildings throughout Portugal. A notable example can be seen in Santarém, where the Graça church has a deeply recessed portal set into a panelled encasement, as in Batalha. Topping this portal is a large rose window with tracery carved from a single block of stone. This church also has a very fine nave and contains a wealth of funerary monuments and tombstones, including that of the navigator Álvares Cabral, who discovered Brazil. Most notable, however, is the tomb of Dom Pedro de Meneses, first governor of Ceuta, which bears the recumbent effigies of the count and his wife resting upon a sarcophagus supported by eight finely sculptured lions.

Like Batalha, Lisbon's Carmo church rose in remembrance of Portugal's victory over the Castilians. Erected between 1393 and 1423 on a hill above the river Tagus, this church, which was for many years one of the largest in the city, incorporated a number of features drawn from the monastery. Unfortunately, however, in 1755 the vaulting collapsed and the interior was gutted by fire; today, the grey bulk of the roofless church, its bare arches pointing at the sky, remains an impressive ruin. It is Lisbon's most striking reminder of the destruction wrought by the great earthquake.

Finally, the cathedral of Guarda, was begun under the influence of Batalha in 1390, but it was not completed until the midfifteenth century, when, again as in Batalha, Manueline decorative features were added to the building.

Although, like Batalha, this cathedral is crowned with Gothic pinnacles and trefoils, its massive towers and sturdier looking flying buttresses give it a somewhat heavier look. The unusual main façade has a Manueline portal and a simple rose window flanked by two large octagonal bell towers. Within, a remarkable multiribbed vault covers the transept crossing, whereas the choir is dominated by a four-level Renaissance altarpiece in gilded *Ançã* stone. This is the famous white limestone of the Coimbra region, which was highly prized by sculptors because it carves as easily as wood. This work of art in high relief contains over one hundred figures in scenes representing the lives of Christ and the Virgin Mary.

The church at Viana do Alentejo, attached to a wall of the town's castle, is an unusual example of a Gothic fortified church displaying a variety of stylistic influences. Here the crenelated exterior has Gothic flying buttresses topped by pinnacles and boasts a lavishly carved Manueline portal, whereas the three-aisled interior is covered with caissoned vaults reflecting the influence of Moorish decorative taste, a fashion which, in the sixteenth century, culminated in the artwork known as *Mudejar*.

THE MANUELINE EXTRAVAGANCE

In the fifteenth century Portugal was finally at peace: the Moors had been definitely vanquished and Castile had temporarily recognized the nation's right of independence. Now, more than ever before, Portugal's unique geographic situation came to play a decisive role in shaping the future. The Iberian peninsula juts out into the Atlantic Ocean, isolated from the rest of Europe behind the high mountain barrier of the Pyrenees. Facing the great ocean on the west, Portugal is dwarfed, on the east, by neighboring Spain — which in the fifteenth century was emerging as a fearful power led by Castile — geographical barrier separates the two. Given these circumstances, the Portuguese understood that if they were to expand their commercial relations and at the same time safeguard their independence from Spain, they must first conquer the sea.

Meanwhile, fifteenth-century Europe saw her trade with the East being strangled by the ever-threatening growth of the Ottoman Empire, whose hostile borders now blocked Marco Polo's famous land route to China and menaced Italy's trade monopoly in the Mediterranean. Silks, drugs, precious stones, and other Oriental goods had stopped flowing into the continent, but the importance of these luxuries was relatively small by comparison to that of spices. Because fresh meat was unavailable during the winter in medieval Europe, all condiments that could be used to preserve meat were in great demand; with the major exception of salt, most of these — pepper, cinnamon, nutmeg, cloves, and ginger — came from the East. It was obvious, therefore, that any nation managing to restore this trade would surely become enormously wealthy.

The hope of discovering a direct sea route to the Spice Islands was one of the motives that led prince Henry the Navigator, son of John I, to establish, on the southwest tip of Portugal, his famous center for the investigation of seafaring knowledge. There he gathered Portugal's best navigators, geographers, astronomers, and shipbuilders and organized expeditions to fill in the gaps in the existing information. By 1446, his explorers had set up colonies in the Azores and Madeira, and, sailing along the west coast of Africa, passed Cape Bojador (in 1434), the edge of the then-known world. Thus they disproved the widespread belief that, south of that cape, the sea boiled and the sun could turn a man black. The invention of the sea quadrant in 1456 enabled Henry to envisage long sea journeys far from the sight of land; therefore, shortly after his death in 1460, his seamen reached the southern tip of Africa, which they enthusiastically named the Cape of Good Hope. Back home, Portugal was by that time enjoying a foretaste of the riches to come: over 1,500 pounds of gold and some 10,000 black slaves from West Africa were arriving in Lisbon every year.

The fabled Spice Islands, however, lay beyond Africa. Although they were at first confused by Spain's claim, in 1492, to have found «the Indies» by a westerly sea route, the Portuguese concluded that their neghbours could not have possibly found India. In 1497, therefore, they sent their foremost navigator, Vasco da Gama, to attempt to round the Cape of Good Hope. Da Gama not only succeeded in this but continued his journey across the Indian Ocean to Calicut, thus opening India as well as the entire East to Portuguese commerce. After that, Portugal rapidly planted a tenuous string of fortified bases and trading posts all the way from Lisbon to the distant Spice Islands and also obtained exclusive rights to trade with China and Japan. During the same period, a Portuguese fleet had accidentally discovered the rich land of Brazil in the West. By early sixteenth century, therefore, Portugal had become the first naval and commercial power of the world, and Prince Henry's dream had come true: Lisbon held the key to the lucrative spice trade.

The height of Portugal's sea power, the so-called spice age, coincided with the reign of king Manuel I, «the Fortunate», who assumed the proud title of Lord of the Conquest, Navigation, and Commerce of the East. During his brilliant rule, from 1495 to 1521, Portugal's commercial enterprise knew no limits. Lisbon, the unrivaled center of Oriental trade, was the «Queen of the Tagus», on whose banks gold, ivory, gems, and, above all, spices were sold to merchants from all parts of Europe. The national optimism released by this vast new wealth provided the perfect context for the emergence of a highly original decorative style — the Manueline — inspired by the sea and the passion for discovery.

The Portuguese discoveries had important effects on all of Europe, for this unprecedent influx of geographic knowledge helped to spark the intellectual curiosity that gave rise to the Renaissance. In Portugal, therefore, the Manueline period marks the transition from Gothic medievalism to Renaissance innovation. King Manuel was a patron of the arts and — to display the wealth gained from his overseas possessions — encouraged the rich decoration of his buildings. Consequently, the architectural style bearing his name is essentially one of surface decoration. Manueline architects tended to fall under the influence of the decorative arts, and trade with the East had enlivened the spirit of invention in carving, textile design, and other minor arts. Portugal was indeed the first European country to understand and interpret Oriental art forms. Structurally, however, Manueline buildings remain late Gothic, though they are sometimes characterized by a simplicity of proportion that announces the emerging rationality of the Renaissance. The uniqueness of these buildings, however the novelty that makes their style symbolic of Portugal's oceangoing adventure lies in the profusion of richly carved decoration on doorways, windows, arcades, and sometimes columns. Inspired by the heroic sea voyages and their exotic destinations, Manueline decoration provides a fascinating study in nautical themes intermingled with sea life and tropical flora. Every possible motif that the carver's imagination could conceive in connection with these voyages was used: twisted ropes, cables, loop knots, anchors, seaweeds, coral, pearls, seashells, palms, pineapples, artichokes, laurel leaves, corncobs, and an endless variety of other evocation material. The result, therefore, is sometimes an incredibly rich composition of intricately carved subjects, whose rare exuberance testifies to the pride then sweeping the nation. A number of outstanding artists, equally talented as architects and sculptors, are responsible for creating the Manueline style as it is known today. Mateus Fernandes, whose work in Batalha was mentioned in the previous chapter, was one of these. Also prominent were the Arruda brothers, João de Castilho, and the famous Boytac, a French immigrant whose creative genius gave birth to the first distinctively Manueline building in 1490. This early example is the Church of Jesus, located in the busy seaport of Setúbal, south of Lisbon. Here Boytac first employed several of the decorative features that best characterize the style. This building has the structure of a Gothic hall church, with a plain façade pierced by a sculptured marble portal. Spiralled pinnacles top the wall abutments, and an elegant Manueline window is set into the wall of the chancel. It is the interior, however, that truly inaugurated the style in the late fifteenth century. The vaults are here supported by six highly original pillars, each of which has three intertwisted stone shafts imitating the strands of fiber in a length of rope. Though spiral-fluted columns had already been used elsewhere in Europe, they had never before been sculptured to resemble rope so closely. The nautical theme appears also in the chancel of the church, where the carved vaulting shafts again imitate the cords and ropes used on Henry the Navigator's caravels. A later example of Boytac's work is the parish church of Golegã, near Santarém, which has a peacked façade decorated by an extraordinary portal. The allegorical carving of portals such as this is a major feature of the Manueline style. Typically, the decoration forms a rectangular composition flanked by tall, twisted columns with spiralled pinnacles.

In a niche above the arched doorway stands a statue of the Virgin, surrounded by typically Manueline motifs like artichokes and the ever-present Cross of the Order of Christ, emblem of the order of Portuguese knights who replaced the Templars after the pope, in 1314, dissolved their order. Topping the portal is a small circular window decorated with King Manuel's armorial bearings and two armillary spheres, another popular motif honouring the nautical instrument whose concentric circles permitted navigators to make astronomical observations at sea.

In Lisbon, the south façade is all that remains of the original Church of Conceição Velha, which was felled by the great earthquake of the eighteenth century. The splendid portal of this ill-fated church is set between two richly carved abutments crowned with armillary spheres. It has a large, sculptured tympanum that shows Our Lady of Mercy sheltering King Manuel, his queen, Pope Leo X, and other personages of that age under her mantle. The most ambitious and probably the finest of all Manueline buildings is the grandiose Monastery of the Hieronymites, or Jerónimos. The monastery overlooks the Tagus near the site where the navigator and his fleet had first set sail. Fittingly, it was the wealth gained from the spice trade that helped finance the high cost of its construction, hence the saying that the monastery was «built by pepper». Boytac worked here until 1517, when João de Castilho added much of the lavish decoration and other artists contributed touches of classicism that hint at the Renaissance. The beautiful white marble church is dominated at the west end by an elegant domed bell tower crowned by the insignia of Portugal's overseas expansion: an armillary sphere surmounted by the Cross of the Order of the Knights of Christ. The long galleries west of this are a neo-Manueline addition dating from the nineteenth century. Facing the wide mouth of the river, the sumptuous south portal of the church is richly decorated with carved pinnacles, statues, and statuettes in a florid composition topped by an ornamental spire bearing the Cross of the Order of Christ. A statue of Henry the Navigator stands in a canopied niche between the twin doors, above which a tympanum contains reliefs that represent scenes from the life of St. Jerome, founder of the Hieronymite order of monks. On either side of this portal are two tall decorated windows flanked by pairs of ringed, ropelike columns that taper off to pinnacles, a typical feature of Boytac's work. Interestingly, although Manueline architects made abundant use of the Gothic arch in all its variations, these windows are already in the round-headed form that became a Renaissance feature.

The interior of the church is breathtaking. The soaring nave and aisles, of almost equal hight, reflect highly original treatment of the interior space. The multiribbed vaults that spring from these pillars in a fanlike design resemble the outspread fronds of towering palm trees, recalling the tropical vegetation of Portugal's colonies. The nave of Jerónimos, on the other hand, is not separated from the aisle because the pillars are very slender and the vault stretches from wall to wall like a huge umbrella. Decorative bosses adorn the intersections of the vaulting framework; a magnificent star vault covers the transept crossing. Like the chapter house vault in Batalha, this remarkable star vault, which seems to hover in midair with no central support, is among the outstanding architectural feats of its day. Despite its bold design, it is also one of the few great vaults in the Lisbon area to have whithstood the earthquake of 1755. Near the west doorway are the nineteenth-century neo-Manueline tombs of Vasco da Gama, and the poet Luís de Camões, author of *The Lusiads*, and epic narration of da Gama's voyage to India and a literary classic. Unfortunately it is not kown whether the remains in the poet's tomb are truly his.

The monastery's display of masterly craftmanship culminates in the lavishly decorated cloister, which is a Manueline masterpiece of dazzling sculptural richness. In contrast with the cloisters at Batalha, this cloister has two stories with round rather than pointed arcade openings. The large openings of the lower gallery, designed by Boytac, are filled in with fretted marble arches supported by small, delicately carved columns; those on the upper story, decorated by João de Castilho, have cusped arches resting on single pinnacled shafts. Remarkable for its perfect unity of style, the whole cloister is alive with Manueline decorations: parapets are lined with reliefs representing interlaced plants evenly interspersed with the Cross of the Order of Christ; piers are covered with evocative motifs, including parrots and exotic birds; and pinnacled buttresses, carved with pearls set in spirals, appear to be held by an ornamental cord. A cornice bearing medallions and decorative rhombi completes the stonework fantasy. One of the architectural wonders of Portugal, this magnificent cloister is especially beautiful in the late afternoon, when the carved stone is washed in a mellow golden light.

As mentioned in an earlier chapter, the hilltop Convent of Christ, in Tomar, combines several architectural styles. This vast complex, which includes seven cloisters and numerous buildings, was the seat of the powerful order of the Knights of Christ, whose proud emblem was carried by the caravels on the voyages of discovery. The Knights of Christ reached the peak of their glory during the Manueline period, when King Manuel, in gratitude for their service, gave the convent a church of noble distinction, built as a continuation of the twelfth-century rotunda of the Templars. This unusual church has a laboriously carved south portal by João de Castilho, which reveals the strong influence of the Plateresque style then popular in Spain, the artist's native country. In contrast with pure Manueline carving, which is deep-cut and produces a strong chiaroscuro effect, Plateresque surface decoration is finely chiselled in low relief and uses a number of classical elements. The ornate Manueline window on the west façade clearly shows the difference between the two; it is, in fact, the most stunning expression of the Manueline style in Portugal. Designed by Diogo de Arruda in 1510, this window has a stone frame carved with a riot of sea-related forms. Here one sees ropes, chains, cables, and seaweeds entangled with two coralencrusted masts standing at the sides of the opening. The frame itself appears to rest on the shoulders of a small bust of the bearded artist, over whose head one recognizes the roots of an oak tree. This tree provided the precious timber that the caravels needed to withstand the stresses of their journeys to the Indian Ocean. The whole fantastic composition is crowned by the emblems of the king and his knights: a royal shield surmounted by the Cross, flanked on either side by armillary spheres fixed on coral branches of the Order de Christ. The extraordinary stonework surrounding the entire window provides a marvellous picture of Portugal's obsession with the sea. The façade on which it is set faces a small cloister and has similar sea-inspired decorations on moldings and buttresses, while the famous window is moored by cables to side turrets. In sharp contrast, a large Renaissance cloister partially covers one side of the Manueline church.

Equally distant from the purity of Gothic and from the Renaissance ideal that detail should be subordinated to unity, the Manueline was a style vividly suggesting the exuberant vitality of King Manuel's Portugal. Commercial contacts with Flanders and the East had brought northern and Oriental influences; these then merged with the Islamic and Christian traditions of medieval Portugal. Manueline decoration is thus a strange sylistic blend, indiscriminately combining Flamboyant Gothic and Moorish motifs and transformed by Portugal's own fascination with the sea and the riches carried across it. The Manueline passion for detailed exuberance, however, was almost certainly inherited from the Moors. Ever since the end of the reconquest, the Moors' artistic refinement had become something of an obsession with the Christian artists of both Portugal and Spain. The marked tendency toward ornament that is now part of the Iberian heritages, can be traced back to this early admiration of Moorish art, whose sensuous forms were often borrowed by the Christians. Manueline decoration bears the stamp of Moorish influence in the form of lacy fretwork mixed with floral motifs as well as round arches and doorways; the portal at the church of Alvor is a good example of the latter. During the Manueline period there was also a rebirth of certain Islamic techniques in the artwork known as *Mudejar*. The term *Mudejar* derives from the Arabic word meaning «subjugated» and referring to the persistence of Islamic art under the Christian yoke. Probably the most beautiful aspect of the *Mudejar* is the use of decorative inlaid woodwork on ceilings. Remarkably fine examples of this can be seen in the churches of São Bento (in Bragança), Escarigo, and Caminha; their ceilings incorporate raised fillets that outline sunken geometrically shaped panels.

THE RENAISSANCE ORDER

IMPROVED education and a rising level of literacy throughout Europe also had the effect of stimulating intellectual curiosity. This new spirit of inquiry, spurred partly by Portugal's astounding geographical discoveries, prompted medieval thinkers to start reexamining their views of the world and to question the Church's authority in the realm of the secular. Christian dogma taught that man's life on earth was secondary to his future after death. This view was challanged when, in the fifteenth century, a number of influential scholars discovered in the ancient literatures of Greece and Rome a wealth of writings supporting the importance of man as individual. These new ideas gave rise to a trickle of humanist sentiment that, over the years, swelled into a torrent of new thought. Originating in Italy — which, as center of the fallen Roman Empire, was the natural home of classicism — the influence of antiquity was first manifested in the writings of Petrarch and Boccaccio. But it soon spread from literature to all fields of human endeavor, including art and architecture. The consequent transformation of medieval Europe was seen as a revival or «renaissance» of the classical spirit.

The development of a classical style in architecture spread across western Europe by means of pattern books explaining the proportions of the ancient Roman prototypes. Through such books, architects everywhere could imitate the style of antiquity merely by studying the drawings and designs published by the leading Italian architects. In this manner Bramante and Palladio, for example, came to have a far-reaching influence on sixteenth-century European architecture. Their work revived the traditional classical orders and renewed the desire for symmetry and purity of line. In Portugal, the classicizing spirit of the Renaissance appeared sporadically during the Manueline period. At first this took the form of decorative work. Architects shuch as João de Castilho thus employed classical ornamental motifs alongside the Flamboyant Manueline decoration then in favour. The medallions and busts at the cloister of Jerónimos date from this early stage, as does the Plateresque main portal of the Convent of Christ. Classical motifs gradually displaced Gothic forms as the new decorative grammar of the Renaissance won acceptance. The French sculptor Nicholas Chantarenne completed the beautiful alabaster altarpiece of the Convent of Pena, in Sintra, by 1532. The figures in this remarkable example of Renaissance sculpture already show the detailed realism of Roman statuary. Likewise, the sculptor Jean de Rouen, who arrived in Portugal soon after Chanterenne, produced several masterworks in Coimbra, most notably the north portal of the Old Cathedral. More monumental structures in the new style were not built in Portugal until after 1550, when the kingdom's commercial power began to decline and King John III discouraged the costly overdecoration of the Manueline style. Change nevertheless came slowly first, since the nation remained wrapped in the golden aura of the Manueline age and was reluctant to abandon its splendor.

Short-lived though it was, the Portuguese Renaissance produced a number of Italian buildings of outstanding quality. The Portuguese humanist Francisco de Holanda, whose years of study in Italy are reflected in his literary work, was largely responsible for the introduction of Italian Classicism into Portugal. His ideas greatly influenced Diogo de Torralva, Portugal's foremost architect of the mid-sixteenth century. Torralva's work at the Great Cloister of the Convent of Christ, built between 1557 and 1566, helped to make this the finest example of High Renaissance architecture in Portugal. His remarkable design combines architectural themes drawn from Bramante, Palladio, and Serlio. Following the classical tradition, giant Doric columns flank the rounded openings of the lower gallery. Upon these, on the upper story, are superimposed columns of the Ionic order. This finely articulated courtyard has rather unusual corners marked by cylindrical stair enclosures that break the angles convexly. A similar if simple intention can be seen in the cut corners adopted by Boytac in the cloister of Jerónimos years earlier.

A short distance away from the Convent of Christ, also in Tomar, stands another outstanding example of classical design. The small Chapel of the Conception, begun about 1530, has a basilican plan with three barrel-vaulted naves separated by Corinthian columns. The interior is well lit by twelve pedimented windows, and the vaults are decorated with raised geometrical motifs. It has been suggested that the chapel, one of the first examples of the

High Renaissance in Portugal may originally have been designed«to point the way out of the Manueline heritage». Despite Torralva, however, the pure Italian classicism of the High Renaissance did not strike deep roots in Portugal, which lacked a strong classical tradition. For this reason, by the end of the sixteenth century, there arose a preference for the greater freedom and variety of form allowed by Italian mannerism. This latter style, which characterized the late Renaissance throughout western Europe, remained classical in derivation while at the same time gradually freeing itself from close adherence to classical rules and proportions. This period of transition in architecture coincided, on the other hand, with the realization of Portugal's worst historic fear: the loss of independance from Spain. The fateful event occured when, following young King Sebastian's death in 1578, Philip II of Spain inherited the Portuguese throne. The consequent union of the two Iberian nations marked the end of Portuguese sea power and broke Lisbon's lucrative monopoly of trade with the Orient.

During the period of Spanish domination from 1581 to 1640, court life moved from Lisbon to Madrid and a certain decadence became evident in all arts. Nonetheless, in 1582, one year after his coronation in Tomar, Philip II ordered the construction of the monumental Church of Saint Vincent without the Walls (São Vicente de Fora), so called because it stands outside the old city walls of Lisbon. Designed by the Italian architect Filippo Terzi, the building reflects the severe majesty favoured by the Spanish monarch. It remains uncertain whether Juan de Herrera, the builder of the Escorial (Philip's famous monastery-palace outside Madrid) participated in the project. The church's harmonious façade employs many of the decorative motifs of true classicism but is clearly mannerist in its free interpretation of the classical order. Terzi modelled the interior after that of Il Gesu' in Rome; it has a spacious single nave and an unusually large chancel. These functional characteristics, first imposed by the Jesuits to facilitate preaching at the time of the Counterreformation, were to be copied in churches throughout Portugal in the seventeenth century. Today, the huge chancel in St. Vincent's contains a beautiful baroque altar; it is set under a richly ornamented canopy topped by statues of saints, and a fine baroque organ of the eighteenth century, one of the finest in the peninsula, was set up on the east wall.

This imposing building, the New Cathedral (Sé Nova) in Coimbra, begun in 1598, also suffered the influence of the so-called Jesuit style of Il Gesu'. It has a flat façade deriving from that of Saint Vincent's in Lisbon, although it is much less classical. Here the structure is surmounted by curved and broken pediments, and side scrolls connect the upper section to the wider lower story. These mannerist features impart a sense of movement not present at Saint Vincent's. The bell towers are pushed back behind the line of the façade, thus lending the frontal view a feeling of perspective that reflects the growing tendency towards greater visual play and heralds the baroque style.

THE BAROQUE SPLENDOR

It may be said that art, having the power to reach the mind and emotions, is another voice of philosophy. As such it was influenced by the rebirth of humanism in the fifteenth century, which paved the way from the Gothic tradition to a rediscovery of the classical spirit. Similarly, the shattering religious confrontation of the sixteenth and seventhenth centuries gradually changed Europe's way of thinking and ultimately also its arts.

As the intellectual ferment of the Renaissance period declined, there ensued an era of ideological warfare — the Reformation and Counterreformation — during which propaganda became something of a psychological weapon. Thus, while the Protestants used the printed word to propagate their revolutionary doctrines, their opponents sought to reinvigorate Catholicism by means of a new kind of propaganda that appealed directly to the emotions. With respect to this, the famous Portuguese historian Oliveira Martins observes, in his *History of the Iberian Civilisation*, that the proponents of the Counterreformation were the first to discover the true principle of educating man: «to build up a sensuous atmosphere of the mind which might give birth to ideas, suitably to preface the material in which to mould and fashion thoughts.» Hence, while Protestants disapproved of all forms of ostentation, the Roman Church came to favour sumptuously decorated buildings both to advertise its spiritual message and to attract new followers. From this enthusiasm for pomp and ostentation was born the elaborate baroque style, given to the use of theatrical effects and optical illusions with which to transport the mind beyond earthly concerns to the world of the spirit. That is, the baroque used form primarily as a means of stirring the soul.

The word «baroque» is believed to derive from the Portuguese *barroco*, a term used to designate the large, irregularly shaped pearls then used in making lavish jewelry. This analogy refers to the curvilinear shapes of the style for the baroque, though classical in derivation, displays a sensuous freedom of movement that tends to treat architecture plastically. Its plethora of visual effects is eminently suited to the Latin temperament of southern Europe, where the philosophy of the Counterreformation and the Roman Church ultimately triumphed over Protestantism.

Portugal, tucked away in the southwest corner of Europe, was one of the bastions of the Counterreformation. Nevertheless, Portuguese religious architecture cultivated a sober Italianate, late-Renaissance style until late in the seventeenth century. Church façades were characteristically flat and relied on side scrolls and broken pediments to impart some sense of movement, as in the New Cathedral (Sé Nova) in Coimbra. Not until 1682 was the first manifestly baroque structure erected in Lisbon. This was the monumental Church of Santa Engrácia, which — in opposition to the mannerist linearism then still popular in Portugal — was the first to employ the sinuous, undulating contours characteristic of pure baroque. Designed by João Antunes, its unusual centralized plan and curving walls, however exercised little influence elsewhere in Portugal, which was to reflect the strong influence of mannerism for decades to come. The church was left unfinished for years, its central dome not being completed until 1966. Although only two centralized plan churches precede Santa Engrácia: Nossa Senhora do Bom Sucesso (Lisbon, 1626) and the Piedade Church (Santarém, 1644), a few interesting examples dated from the eighteenth century did follow this precedent. These are the Church of Bom Jesus da Cruz, in Barcelos, designed by João Antunes in 1705, the Senhor das Barrocas church in Aveiro, begun in 1722, and the unfinished Church of Senhor da Pedra, begun in 1740 near Óbidos, which adopts an unusual hexagonal plan. They are however exceptions to the national rule.

It was hence not in architecture so much as in the decorative arts that a native baroque style came to evolve and find complete expression. Portugal's latent love for ornament, which was manifested so vigorously in the decoration of the Manueline style, rapidly revived after the restoration of independence from Spain in 1640. Wood became the preferred material, as it is more readily carved than stone and has the warmth that best lends itself to the expression of baroque themes; wood was, moreover, in abundant supply at the time, including precious woods imported from Brazil and the African colonies. Therefore Portuguese baroque art initially took the form of richly ornamented carved wooden altarpieces. These first appeared in the mannerist churches of the mid-seventeenth century and presumably imitated the architecture of church portals, being flanked by columns set under an arch. With the introduction of the spiralling column, however their composition became more dynamic and began to reflect a genuine baroque vitality not yet matched by the churches' exteriors. Once the carving was complete, the entire surface of the altarpiece was encrusted with gold, for gold was felt to have the soul-stirring power sought by the leaders of the Counterreformation. In this way the highly specialized art known in Portugal as *talha dourada* (gilt woodcarving) came into being. It, together with the ubiquitous Portuguese *azulejo,* gave rise to a native style of rare beauty and originality. An early example of Portuguese baroque decoration can be seen at the Church of Camarate, near Lisbon: here the chancel displays a profusion of intricately carved *talha dourada,* while the nave walls retain their original sixteenth century green-and-white *azulejos.* The ceiling is decorated with large panelled paintings.

By the late seventeenth century, the *azulejo* had become an indispensable complement to the religious and secular architecture in Portugal. Occasionally, church interiors were entirely covered with glazed tiling, as in the Church of St. Lawrence (São Lourenço) in Almansil, where the blue-and-white *azulejos* confer a radiance of rare intensity upon the tiny interior. This superb little church is an excellent example of the enormous popularity of this decorative element — attributable to the fact that it was economical, virtually indistructible and was easy to clean while at the same time adding colour and luster. As a distinctive ingredient of Portuguese baroque decoration, the tiled panels seen in so many of the country's churches (as well as its homes and gardens) played a role similar to that of mural paintings in Italy. In fact, Portuguese architecture never adopted the oval plan of pure Italian baroque largely because it was committed to the long, flat surfaces so eminently suited to tiled decoration. The demand for *azulejos* became so great that on occasions tiles had to be imported from Holland to satisfy the market. There exist two magnificent examples of early baroque Portuguese interiors decorated with Dutch tiles: the Church of Nossa Senhora da Conceição dos Cardais, in Lisbon, with tiling signed by J. van Oort of Amsterdam, probably dating from 1698; and the Parish Church in Nazaré, which has tiles signed by W. van Kloet, delivered in Lisbon in 1709. Throughout the seventeenth century Portuguese *azulejos* repeated floral motifs and eventually came to use a third colour — yellow. Under the influence of the Dutch, Portuguese tile masters also strived to obtain richer blues. A remarkable example of Dutch blue-and-white tiling can be seen in the Lisbon Church of Madre de Deus.

Portuguese baroque art culminated during the reign of King John V (1698-1750). Under his rule, the discovery of gold and diamonds in Brazil brought new riches into the royal treasury; part of this vast wealth remained in Portugal, where it sparked a new age of prosperity and stimulated the arts in Portugal.

As was to be expected, the discovery of Brazilian gold immediately affected the development of *talha dourada,* for it increased the supply and lowered the price of gold leaf. The gilded woodwork — which, as in Camarate, was initially restricted to individual alterpieces — was now given a free rein: it invaded the church chancel and began to creep into the nave, covering it all with gold. Thus was born the concept of the «golden church», which became immensely popular in Portugal and Brazil in the eighteenth century. Predictably, the unbelievably rich interiors that now evolved often surpassed the artistic challange posed by the Counterreformation, whereby the Church sought to «build up a sensuous atmosphere of the mind».

The finest examples of the «golden church» ideal are found in the north of Portugal, for this region had scarcely been touched by the Renaissance and was therefore more open to the excesses of the baroque style. Of these northern churches, the best known are the Church of St. Francis (São Francisco) and that of St. Claire (Santa Clara) in the city of Oporto. In both, but especially in St. Francis, the interior walls covered with such a giddy whirl of gilded enrichment that the eyes yearn in vain for an instant's repose. In St. Francis, the interior's original Gothic structure has been all but obliterated by the frenzied baroque ornamentation: carved flowers, birds, flying angels, and golden vines emerge from the shadows, seeming to foreshadow the sensuous pleasures that await the faithful in heaven. The lighting is purposefully controlled, since it was understood that the intrinsic drama of gold work increases proportionally with the depth of the surrounding darkness. Although the Gothic exterior bears on its main façade a fine baroque portal with columns, it is the interior decoration that, like St. Claire's, best reflects the spirit of the style. These incredibly overornamented interiors, almost every inch of them covered with gold leaf, must have appeared magical indeed to the worshippers who first beheld them.

Equally successful if somewhat more restrained examples of eighteenth-century *talha dourada* abound throughout Portugal. The interior of the Convent of Jesus, in Aveiro, is particularly noteworthy for the richness of its gilded woodwork, which here combines with the convent's wealth of bronze and marble sculpture to create an overall scheme of extravagant beauty. In Braga, the interior of the city's romanesque cathedral was profoundly transformed by the introduction of two magnificent baroque organs. These are sumptuously decorated with allegorical wood carvings and like many other organs in Portugal and in Spain, some of the pipes are laid out horizontally; these are known as *en chamade*. The organ lofts, which are backed by beautifully carved and gilded choir stalls, are connected by a humpbacked bridge with a handsome balustrade. Because organ music contributed effectively to the baroque era's wish to stir the emotions, other impressive organs were now installed in many of Portugal's major churches; outstanding examples include those in the Cathedral of Oporto and in the Paulistas Church in Lisbon.

In his day, King John V was one of the wealthiest monarchs in Europe. The riches brought back from Brazil enabled him to initiate a number of costly building projects, the most ambitious of which was the immense monastery-palace of Mafra, not far north of Lisbon. Designed by the king's German-born architect Johann Friederich Ludwig and completed in 1730, this monumental marble edifice, with 4500 doors and windows, betrays the architect's academic training in Rome. Opening onto a large open square, the church's harmonious façade has a central pediment flanked by very tall belfries. One of the finest domes in Portugal, coffered and lavishly painted on the inside, tops the transept crossing and dominates the monastery. The interior is spacious and well propotioned but, like the exterior, makes no major concessions to Portuguese taste. For this reason its architectural influence was ultimately confined to Lisbon and the Alentejo. Mafra nevertheless served as a training school for a new generation of artisans and remains today an important repository of Italian and Portuguese sculpture. Alessandro Giusti, an Italian sculptor of repute, directed the monastery's famous school of sculpture between 1753 and 1770. Ludwig, known in Portugal as Ludovice, is also believed to have participated in the decoration of the Church of the Mother of God (Madre de Deus) in Lisbon, commissioned by John V in the early eighteenth century. Here, however, the final result was a typically Portuguese combination of *talha dourada, azulejos*, and painting. Built on white marble, the single nave is lined with large panels of glazed blue-and-white tiles, while the upper walls and barrel-vaulted ceiling are decorated with religious paintings in gilt frames. But surely the most extravagant project undertaken under the patronage of King John V was that involving the small Chapel of St. John the Baptist. This chapel, one of the most costly structures of its size ever built, is entirely carved from semiprecious stones such as alabaster, jasper, lapis lazuli and agate, being further enriched with marble sculpture, gold work, and bronze. Built with help of more than one hundred artists in Vanvitelli's workshops in Rome, the chapel was shipped to Portugal by order of the Portuguese monarch in 1747, where it was reassembled over a two-year period inside Lisbon's Church of São Roque.

Meanwhile in the north, an Italian-born architect named Niccoló Nasoni introduced, a genuine structural baroque based on Italian precedents. Nasoni's famous Clerigos Church, in Oporto, is thus the first church in Portugal built on an oval plan — a rarity in a country so strongly reluctant to abandon the rectangular concept. Nevertheless, his architecture, unlike Ludwig's, adapted successfully to Portuguese taste and tradition, a fact perhaps best reflected in his work at Casa de Mateus in Vila Real, one of Portugal's splendid baroque residences. The palace chapel is here housed in a handsome building harmoniously annexed to the east end of the palace; on its exterior, the combination of whitewash and dark, sculptured granite, effectively exemplifies the taste of that time. It has broken pediment and finials, but as a palace chapel it remains somewhat unusual in that it does not form an integral part of the palace itself.

The trend favouring elaborately decorated façades culminated in the region of Braga, where it gave rise to a native adaptation of the rococo style then popular in Central Europe. This development is well illustrated by the Church of S. Mary Magdalene (Santa Maria Madalena) in Falperra, designed by André Soares da Silva in 1750. The church façade displays a combination of drapery and writhing plant motifs that seem to grow out of the doors and windows and to hang from the projecting cornices. Here again the decoration is carved in dark granite and set off against luminous whitewash. Woodwork decoration, on the other hand, also came under the influence of the new style, especially through prints of rococo work in Bavaria. An instance of this can be seen in the superb altarpiece at the Monastery Church of Tibães, also in the vicinity of Braga. Its garlanded columns are unusual in that they are set upon Oriental-looking pedestals, probably inspired by the fashion, then current in Europe for Chinese art and ceramics.

In some cases Portuguese designers felt the need to extend the theatrical of the baroque style into the field of landscaping. This is exemplified by the pilgrimage churches, most of which by tradition, were built on remote hilltops in northern Portugal. In the eighteenth century, the idea arose that these venerated shrines deserved more fitting approaches than the dusty paths by which they were then approached. The baroque solution was to provide series of terraced stone staircases set dramatically into the hillsides. This idea was carried out for a number of pilgramage churches in Portugal and in Brazil, of which the grandest is the Sanctuary of Bom Jesus do Monte, outside Braga. Its approach also best complements the church's natural setting. Here one reaches the sanctuary by a succession of richly sculptured baroque staircases that rise majestically through the surrounding of trees.

The perspective is ingenious: it sweeps uphill in a series of zigzagging granite lines punctuated by sculpture, leading the eye upon elaborate vista to the twin-towered church at the top. Built in ascending platforms the stairway is accompanied along its entire route by figure sculpture, allegorical fountains and small chapels representing the Stations of the Cross. The first and lower portion of the staircase was begun in 1723 by order of the Bishop of Braga, Dom Rodrigo de Moura Teles. When the Bishop died in 1728, the second portion, known as «the staircase of the five senses», was already under construction but was not completed until 1774. The third and final portion of the staircase, known as «the virtues», is the work of the architect Cruz Amarante, who also supplied the plans for the neoclassical church that crowns the whole project. Begun in 1784, the church was not finished for lack of funds until a generous donor made possible its completion only in 1837.

Other famous pilgrimage churches include that of Nossa Senhora dos Remédios, in Lamego, and Senhora da Peneda, in a remote mountainous area on the far north. The baroque staircase in Lamego, some 500 steps long, climbs first to a terrace with a theatrical set of columns bearing biblical figures, from where it proceeds uphill to the eighteenth century church. Even longer is the staircase at Senhora da Peneda, which leads up to a church built against a huge block of granite.

Portugal was at the height of her new prosperity when, in November 1755, a devastating earthquake struck Lisbon. It hit the city and its suburbs with such violence that the work of many centuries was put to waste in minutes during which more than ten thousand people were either killed of mortally injured. Of Lisbon's fine churches, only the Monastery Church of Jerónimos survived virtually unscathed; all the rest were totally or partially ruined.

During the following years vast reconstruction efforts were undertaken, pushed largely by the iron-willed Marquis of Pombal, Portugal's prime minister.

Under his brilliant guidance, a group of outstanding engineers and architects set about the colossal task of repairing the damage and, most importantly rebuilding the entire city center. Under the circumstance — which called for speed, efficency, and economy — there was a strong reaction against the costly overornamentation of the baroque style. As a result, the rebuilding program prompted a marked return to seventeenth century rationalism and linearity confirming the rise of neoclassicism. New buildings thus came under the classicizing influence of the Monastery of Mafra, in whose school many of the new artists had been trained. Chief among the new generation of architects was Mateus Vicente, who designed the monumental Estrela Basilica in Lisbon. This dignified, homogeneous building which echoes the formality and symmetry of form previously expressd by Ludwig in Mafra. Begun in 1779 and completed ten years later, the basilica has a well-balanced neoclassical façade with twin bell towers, a central pediment, and an imposing dome at the crossing visible behind. Although the building incorporates touches of baroque ornamentation, especially in the upper parts of the belfries, it has an overall simplicity of design that is more in keeping with the burgeoning neoclassicism. As Lisbon's last great church, it is a grandiose final expression of the country's long and immensely rich history in religious architecture.

Historical events in the early nineteenth century put an end to the age of great religious building in Portugal. The Napoleonic invasions and the flight of the royal family to Brazil were followed by a period of civil strife. At the end of this, in 1834, a liberal decree banished all religious orders and appropriated their possessions taking them into the national treasury. Moreover, when the royal family returned to Portugal in 1821, the crown no longer held the autocratic power whereby in the past it had indulged in costly projects either to immortalize the accomplishments of a reign (Batalha, Jerónimos) or to commemorate the birth of a long-awaited dynastic heir (Mafra, Estrela). Religion had ceased to be the nation's vitalizing force and the great patrons of religious art were stripped of their historic powers.

To say that Portugal has made a significant contribution to the evolution of our modern world is an understatement. Indeed it was Portugal that, during the age of discovery, first revealed the actual shape of our world and opened new horizons to European culture and commerce. Then, two and a half centuries later, it was again Portugal that indirectly financed the early industrial revolution. Portuguese history thus lies at the foundations of the modern age. And, as one of the world's great civilizing forces, this history finds its richest expression in those of its buildings that honour God: namely, its churches. Each of these historic shrines is therefore reflection of its era, representing, so to speak, a thread in the fabric of world history. The photographs accompanying this text capture, in visual terms, this beauty and variety which is Portugal's legacy to the people of today.

São Frutuoso.
The Visigothic funerary chapel showing Byzantine influence.

Lourosa.
The Visigothic simplicity of its nave.

Travanca.
Church with defense tower and detail of tower door.

Following page:
Coimbra, Sé Velha.
The finest Romanesque church in Portugal erected between 1140 and 1175, the Cathedral retains the appearance of a fortress, complete with merlons.
The east façade shows the dome and the apsidal chapels.

Coimbra.
Detail of the Romanesque architecture under the dome.

Alterpiece in gilded wood by the Flemish masters Olivier de Gand and Jean d'Ypres.

Lisbon, Sé.
Originally built in the 12C after the town had been captured by the Crusaders. The Cathedral has been remodelled and restored many times.

Detail of the Ambulatory and two details of the vaulting.

Church of Tabuaço.
Romanesque church located in the vicinity of Viseu emphasizing the role of sculpture in the doorways and capitals with animal, geometrical and other motifs.

Church of Bravães.
Detail of the remarkable Romanesque doorway decorated with doves, monkeys, humans and geometrical motifs.

Opposite page:
Igreja de Nossa Senhora da Orada (Melgaço).
Another Romanesque church, showing a pointed arch doorway.

54

Church of Manhente.
Its joining defense tower, Romanesque doorway and geometrical decorative details.

Opposite page:
Ferreira de Aves.
Romanesque doorway and detail of the same door.

Church of Castro de Avelãs.
Its unique apse of possible oriental inspiration totally constructed with bricks making it unique in the Northern region.

Oporto, Sé.
The 13C Romanesque rose window over the Baroque doorway.

The colour stained glass window.

The Portuguese silver altar of the 17C in the Chapel of The Holy Sacrament.

Oporto, Sé.
Detail of cloister.

Detail of twisted serpent on stairway by Niccoló Nasoni.

The 14C Gothic cloister, decorated with «azulejos» illustrating the life of the Virgin and Ovid's Metamorphoses.

The church of Mértola.
This church is based on the original Arabic mosque and shows typical Alentejo cylindrical towers and Muslim merlons.

Church of Mértola.
The ancient «mihrab», a niche, place of prayer for the Muslims.

A general view of the nave with typical Gothic vaulting.

Alcobaça, Monastery of Santa Maria.
The main façade.

Alcobaça.
Central nave and details of striking vertical lines giving a spacious perspective.

*Following page:
The impressive refectory with ribbed vaulting and a stairway surmounted by a colonnade leading to a pulpit.*

Alcobaça.
Hall of Tombs. The unusual consoles sustain some fine Gothic vaulting.

Ornate Manueline doorway leading to the Sacristy.

Alcobaça.
Kings' Hall with terracotta statues representing the Portuguese Kings and a frieze of «azulejos» decorating the lower part of the Hall.

The 14C Cloister of Silence where the Cistercian monks used to meditate and pray.

The monumental kitchen with its open fireplace. Fresh water from the river Alcoa used to run right through.

Alcobaça.
Tombs of Inês de Castro and Dom Pedro in Flamboyant Gothic carved in soft limestone.

A detail from Inês de Castro's tomb representing Judas' kiss.

Alcobaça.
The Last Judgement, scene from Inês de Castro's tomb.

Following page:
Évora, Sé.
Built in 12C and 13C, this church has a granite façade flanked by two massive towers. The top of the walls of the nave and aisles are decorated with crenellation.

Évora, Sé.
View of the pointed dome over the crossing. On the opposite page, the west entrance.

Évora, Sé.
The chancel was remodelled in the 18C by the famous architect Ludovice and the crucifix over the altar is by the sculptor José de Almeida.

Santa Clara-a-Velha, Coimbra.
The ruins of this Gothic church.

Santa Clara-a-Velha.
*Nave showing the effect of the floods
and a detail of the vault.*

Monastery church of Leça do Bailio.
Built in granite with its tall classic Gothic battlemented tower and the courtyard showing the south entrance.

Leça do Bailio.
Details of the church tower showing the pyramid shaped merlons and the capitals. On the opposite page, the nave.

Following page:
Batalha, Our Lady of Victory.

Batalha.
An aisle and chapel illuminated by the multicoloured stained glass window and a view of the nave with its sweeping vaulting.

Batalha.
*The Founder's Chapel with the tomb of Dom João I and his wife Philippa of Lancaster. The chapel contains tombs of other royal members including Henry the Navigator.
On the opposite page a detail of the octagonal lantern topped by a star-shaped cupola.*

Batalha.
Details of Manueline sculpture work in the archway leading to the Unfinished Chapels.

Batalha.
Details of rare exuberance of sculptures, possibly of Oriental inspiration.

*Following page:
Three archways in Dom Duarte's «Pantheon» generally referred to as The Unfinished Chapels.*

Batalha.
Two views of the Unifinished Chapels, seven chapels radiate from the octogonal rotunda. On top of the upper part, the famous incomplete pillars.

Batalha.
Sculpture details.

Batalha.
Exterior view of the Unfinished Chapels and a detail from a door.

Batalha.
The Royal Cloister. Here the Manueline and the Gothic style mix most successfully. The shafts of the elegant Manueline columns are adorned with coils, pearls and shell motifs.

Batalha.
Fountain in the Royal Cloister and a detail of the medieval sculpture from the Chapter House.

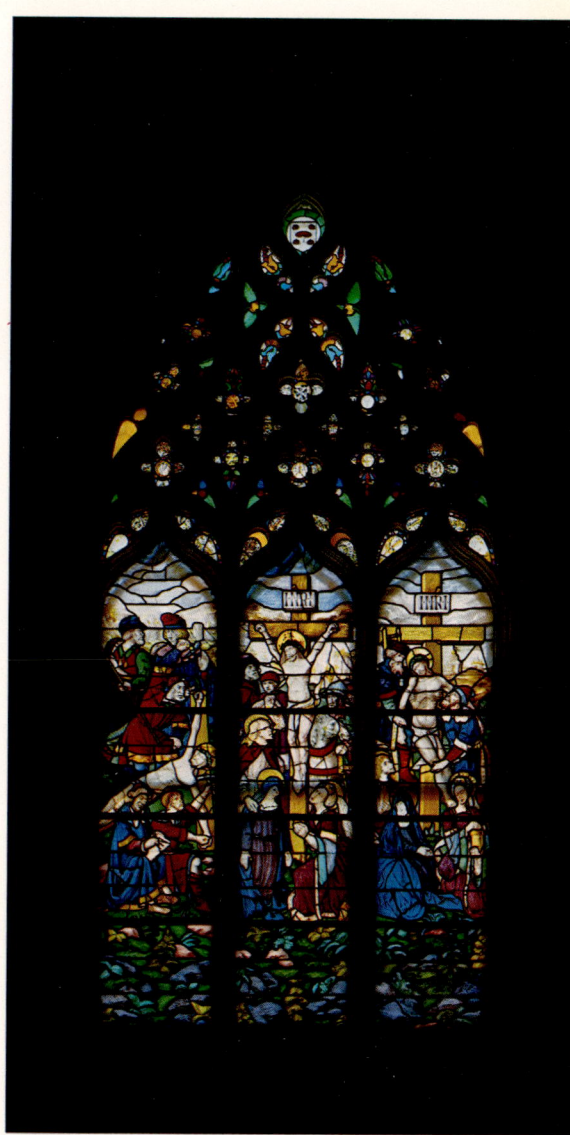

Batalha.
The Chapter House which now houses the Tomb of the Unknown Soldier and the beautiful 16C stained glass window representing scenes from the Passion. Detail of Corbel's sculpture representing Afonso Domingues, architect of the monastery.

Following page:
Guarda, Sé.
This granite edifice was begun in the Gothic style and completed in 1540, it is crowned with pinnacles and trefoils.

Santarém, church of Graça.
A Gothic church dating from 1380; on the façade the panelling over the doorway immediately recalls Batalha. The rose window, which is the finest in the country, has been carved out of a single block of stone. The nave has been restored and below is the 15C tomb of Dom Pedro de Meneses, first governor of Ceuta, upheld by eight lions and carved with leaf motifs and coats of arms.

Following page:
Viana do Alentejo.
*Church and city walls.
The two massive towers are part of the defensive system of the city.*

Guarda, Sé.
The main façade on the opposite page has a Manueline doorway framed by two octagonal towers.

A detail of the Renaissance gilded altarpiece attributed to Jean de Rouen depicting more than one hundred figures.

The northern façade, below, is embellished with a Gothic doorway surmounted by a Manueline window.

Viana do Alentejo

The interior is outstanding for its size and the walls are decorated with 17C «azulejos».

The fine Manueline doorway has a slender twisted central column and the tympanum is decorated with stylized flowers, the pinnacle is flanked by two armillary spheres.

Convent of Carmo, Lisbon.
This church was built at the end of 14C and during the earthquake of 1755 the nave caved in. It is now a memorable ruin with an archeological museum attached.

Church of Jesus, Setúbal.
Designed by Boytac and constructed in Arrábida marble, this church is one of the first examples of Manueline decoration, particularly emphasized by the twisted pillars and the spiral ribs of the vault above the chancel. The walls are partly covered with 17C «azulejos». The doorway is in Flamboyant Gothic.

Three remarkable Manueline doorways: **Church of Golegã, Church of Conceição Velha** *in Lisbon with carvings showing Our Lady of Compassion sheltering Pope Leo X, King Manuel, Queen Leonor, bishops and other personalities of the time beneath her robe and on the opposite page,* **Matriz Church of Batalha.**

Jerónimos Monastery, Lisbon.
This monastery originally designed by Boytac, is considered a jewel of the Manueline art. On the opposite page the south door is a typical composition of sculpture and architecture topped by the Cross of the Order of Christ. Below is a detail of the same door showing a statue of Prince Henry the Navigator.

Jerónimos.
*Nave and vaulting. The interior is outstanding and a daring architectural feat as the network vaulting is of almost equal height over the nave and aisles.
View of the church from the main altar with balcony showing the «coro alto».*

Jerónimos.
The rich sculptured Cloister forms a hollow square and is two stories high. The ground level by Boytac has rich and wide arches as well as decoration carved in the massive walls. The upper level, by João de Castilho, is more delicate in style.

Jerónimos.
A general view of the Cloister with the unusual cut corners and a detail of the fountain with the lion.

Jerónimos.
Details of woodwork from the middle of 16C.

Convent of Christ, Tomar.
The construction of this historical monument began in 12C and was completed in 17C.

The window is the most amazing example of Manueline style. The decoration rises from the roots of an oak tree supported on the bust of what is considered to be the portrait of Diogo de Arruda. See detail.

Tomar.
The church doorway has complex decoration with a clear mixture of Gothic and early Renaissance motifs.

Detail of sculpture from this door.

Following page:
The Manueline nave which King Manuel commissioned to Diogo de Arruda, leading to the Templars' Rotunda or «Charola».

Main cloister.

Tomar.
Two spiral staircases from the main cloister.

Tomar.
The «Charola» or Templars' Rotunda, built in the 12C on the model of the Holy Sepulchre in Jerusalem. The paintings as well as the polychrome wood statues are by Portuguese artists of the 16C.

São Bento, Bragança.
This church is particularly known for its beautiful «Mudejar» ceiling, based as most, on geometrical designs.

Coimbra, Sé Nova.
This austere Baroque church was started at the end of 16C.

Chapel of Nossa Senhora da Conceição, Tomar.
This small chapel is possibly the finest Renaissance piece of architecture built in Portugal.

São Vicente de Fora, Lisbon.
Built by Filippo Terzi at the end of 16C. The church is adorned with life-size wooden sculptures of this period. The cloister walls are magnificently covered with «azulejos».

Detail of canopy.

Santa Engrácia, Lisbon.
Built in 1682, this church officially starts the Baroque in Portugal when it adopts flowing lines seemingly in movement.
This church is now the national pantheon.

São Lourenço, Almansil.
The walls and vaulting of this Baroque church are covered with «azulejos» dating from 1730 depicting the life and martyrdom of this Saint. The brightly coloured tiles are the work of an artist known as Policarpo de Oliveira Bernardes.

Church of Camarate, Lisbon.
A typical church of the early Baroque retaining tiles and paintings. The church also provides us with an early work of an altarpiece.

The Church of Misericordia, Évora.
This is an early example when carved wood work starts invading the nave of the church. The walls are decorated with «azulejos» of 18C.

Conceição Church, Tavira.
Primitive Gothic façade from the south region of Portugal.

Paulistas Church, Lisbon.
Also called Santa Catarina, another good example of carved gilded woodwork of the 17C.

Church of São Francisco, Real (Braga)
Baroque church of 18 C. Next, the Visigothic funerary chapel of São Frutuoso de Montélios.

Paulistas Church.
An impressive organ in this church.
Detail of carved gilded woodwork.

Carmo Church, Tavira.
An example of a polychrome decorated altar from the 18C.

Convent Church of Jesus, Aveiro.
It is now part of a museum. The decoration was completed in 1702. The interior, particularly the chancel, are masterpieces of all the expressions of Baroque exuberance.

Convent Church of Jesus, Aveiro.
Details of the interior.

Following page:
Braga, Sé.
One of the most sumptuously decorated organs of the 18C.

Santa Clara, Oporto.
An important 15C and 16C church with the interior totally covered with richly carved polychrome gilded woodwork.

São Francisco, Oporto.
An originally Gothic church with a fine rose window. The decorative opulence of the interior is considered a triumph of the Baroque richness. The gilded woodcarvings cover the whole church as well as the vaulting. There is also a richness in niches decorated with altar paintings polychrome sculptures and «azulejos».

São Francisco.
Details of paintings and gilded woodwork.

São Francisco.
View of the vaulting from the altar and a general view of the nave.

Casa de Mateus.
One of the finest examples of Baroque architecture showing the adjoining house chapel totally integrated with the house.

Palácio da Pena, Sintra.
The only remains of the monastery in this 19C Palace built around a former 16C Hieronymite monastery are the Manueline cloister and the chapel with this beautiful altar by Nicolas Chanterenne.

The Monastery, Basilica and Palace of Mafra.

Was originally commissioned by King John V to his architect, Ludovice who was helped in completing this enormous task by Portuguese and Italian architects. The Mafra School was founded here as many foreign artists were working on the spot and varied precious stones and materials were imported to embellish this construction.

The Basilica façade, built in marble, is flanked by two wings. The interior is elegant in proportion and richly ornamented.

Following page:
Two views of the Baroque church dome. Four arches at the transept support a magnificent rose and white marble cupola.

Church of Bom Jesus do Monte, Braga.
The richly decorated Baroque monumental staircase leading to the pilgrim church is bordered by chapels with lifesize terracotta figures, fountains and religious scenes in «azulejos».

Santa Maria Madalena Church, Falperra.
This Baroque church has six flanks of steps leading to a sumptuous façade in granite and rocaille work of which a detail is shown.

Monastery Church of Tibães.
An example of rich Baroque church in the North of the country. It has orientally inspired details in the interior which were the fashion at the time.

Madre de Deus Church, Lisbon.
The «coro alto» in this church reflects the 17C decorative style of Portuguese gilded woodwork and paintings.

The nave is also richly decorated adding the element of «azulejos» to the walls.

Detail of «azulejos» decoration.

Basílica da Estrela, Lisbon.
This imposing Baroque basilica was built at the end of 18C, it has a harmonious façade flanked by two towers and is covered by a white and rose cupola surmounted by a lantern tower.

The white marble tomb of Queen Maria I, a work of Faustino José Rodrigues.

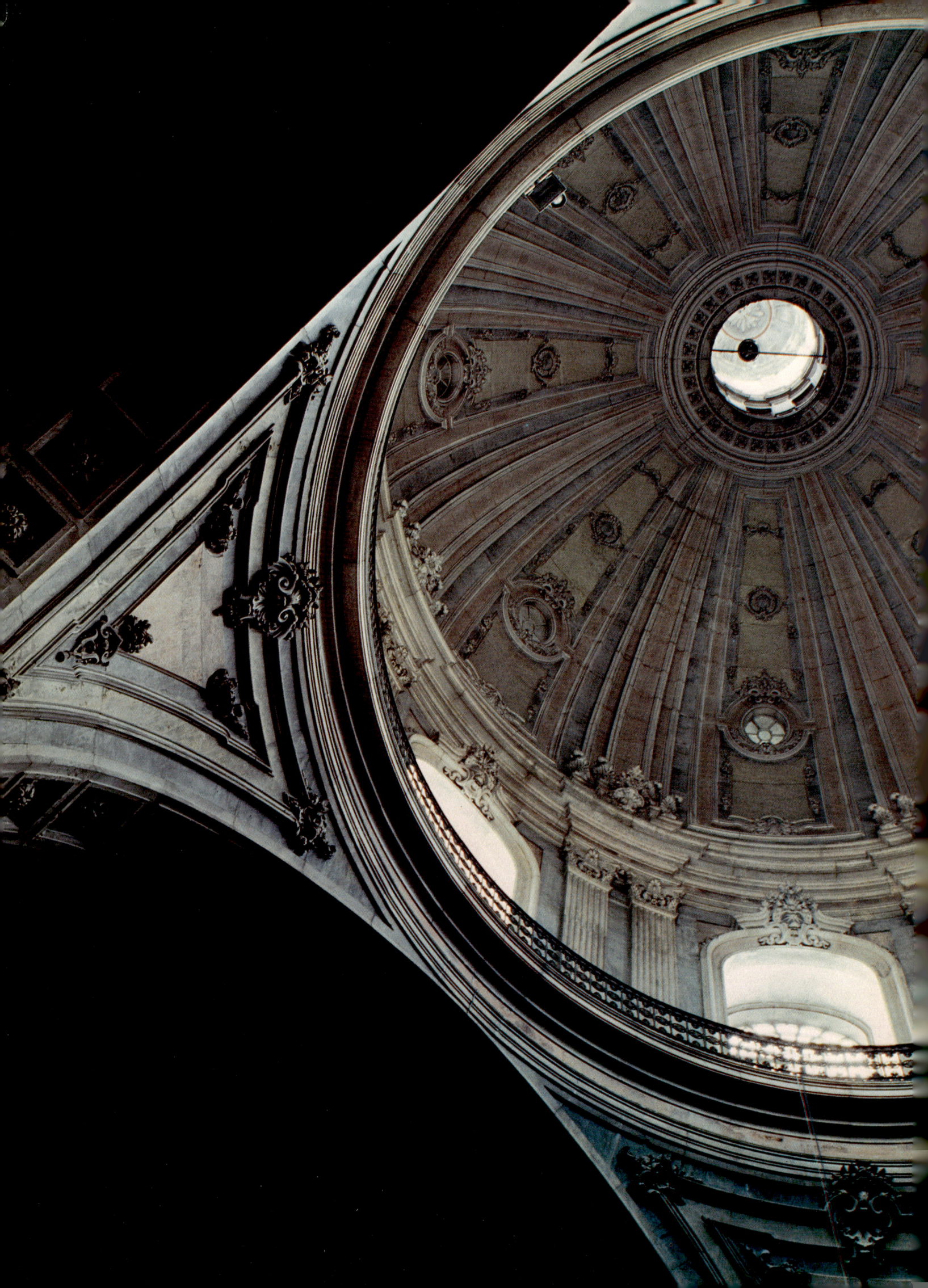

INDEX

Águias, church of São Pedro das — Tabuaço	17, 50, 51	Golegã, church of	28, 128
Amaro de Beja, church of Santo	13	Graça, church of — Santarém	24, 114, 115
Alcobaça, Abbey Church of Our Lady of	19, 20, 21, 64-77	Guarda, Sé	24, 116, 117
Alvor, church of	30	Jerónimos, monastery of — Lisbon	28, 32, 39, 40, 130-139
		Jesus, convent church of the — Aveiro	37, 167, 168, 169
Barrocas, church of Senhor das — Aveiro	35	Jesus, church of — Setúbal	27, 126, 127
Batalha, Matriz Church	129	John the Baptist, chapel of Saint — Lisbon	38
Batalha, Our Lady of Victory	8, 22, 23, 24, 40, 90-113	Lamego, Sé	16
Bento, church of São — Bragança	30, 150, 151	Leça do Bailio, fortress-church of	22, 86, 87, 88, 89
Bom Jesus da Cruz, church of — Barcelos	35	Lisbon, Sé	16, ,48, 49
Bom Jesus do Monte, church of — Braga	39, 186, 187	Lourosa, church of	13, 42
Bom Sucesso, church of Nossa Senhora do — Lisbon	35	Lourenço, church of São — Almansil	36, 158-159
Braga — Sé	16, 37, 170, 171	Madre de Deus, church of — Lisbon	36, 38, 192, 193
Bravães, church of	17, 52	Mafra, monastery of	37, 38, 40, 182-185
		Manhente, church of	17, 55
Camarate, church of	36, 160	Mateus, palace-chapel of the Casa de	38, 180
Caminha, church of	30	Maria Madalena, church of — Falperra	38, 188, 189
Cardais, church of Nossa Senhora da Conceição dos — Lisbon	36	Mértola, church of	60, 61, 62, 63
Carmo, church of — Lisbon	24, 124, 125	Misericórdia, church of — Évora	161
Carmo, church of — Tavira	166	Nazaré, parish church of	36
Castro de Avelãs, church of	54		
Catarina, church of Santa — Lisbon (see also Paulistas church)	37, 163, 164, 165	Oporto, Sé	16, 37, 56, 57, 58, 59
Christ, convent of — Tomar	7, 29, 30, 32, 104-149	Orada, church of Nossa Senhora da — Melgaço	17, 53
Clara-a-Velha, Convent Church of Santa — Coimbra	22, 83, 84, 85	Paulistas church — Lisbon (see also Santa Catarina)	37, 163, 164, 165
Clara, church of Santa — Oporto	37, 172, 173	Pedra, church of Senhor da — Óbidos	35
Clara, church of Santa — Santarém	22	Pedro, church of São — Balsemão	13
Clérigos, church of — Oporto	38	Pena, convent of — Sintra	32, 181
Coimbra, Sé Nova	33, 35, 152	Peneda, pilgrimage church of Senhora da	39
Coimbra, Sé Velha	16, 32, 44, 45, 46, 47	Piedade, church of — Santarém	35
Conceição Velha, church of — Lisbon	28, 128		
Conceição, church of — Tavira	162	Remédios, pilgrimage church of Nossa Senhora dos — Lamego	39
Conceição, chapel of — Tomar	32, 153	Roque, church of São — Lisbon	38
Engrácia, church of Santa — Lisbon	35, 156-157	Roriz, church of	17
Escarigo, church of	30		
Estrela, basílica of — Lisbon	40	Salvador, church of São — Travanca	17, 43
Évora, Sé	16, 21, 78, 79, 80, 81, 82	Tibães, monastery church of	39, 190, 191
Ferreira de Aves, church of	17		
Francisco, church of São — Oporto	37, 54, 174, 179	Vicente de Fora, church of São — Lisbon	33, 154-155
Frutuoso de Montélios, church of São — Braga	13, 42	Viana do Alentejo, parish church	24, 120, 121, 122, 123

BIBLIOGRAPHY

Arte em Portugal, História da (Directed by Aarão de Lacerda, 3 vols., Porto 1942).

Atkinson, William C. — A History of Spain and Portugal (Pelican, Great Britain 1960).

Azevedo, Carlos de — Baroque Organ-Cases of Portugal, Amsterdam 1972.

Bazin, G. — L'Architecture religieuse au Portugal et au Brésil à l'époque baroque, Lisboa 1949.

Bury, John B. — «The Arts in Portugal — Architecture» in Portugal and Brazil, An Introduction Oxford, 1953; Late Baroque and Rococo in North Portugal, in «Journal of the Society of Architectural Historians», 1956.

Chicó, Mário Tavares — O Mosteiro da Batalha e a Arquitectura em Portugal no fim do século XIV e no século XV, in História da Arte em Portugal, Directed by Aarão de Lacerda, 1948; A Catedral de Lisboa e a Arte Portuguesa da Idade Média, in «Belas Artes», n.º 6, Lisboa 1953; A Arquitectura Gótica em Portugal, Lisboa 1954.

Dony, Paul — Batalha (Un problème d'influences), Lisbon 1957

Eça, João M. C. de Almeida — S. Frutuoso de Montélios, XVI Congrès International d'Histoire de l'Art, Lisbonne — Porto, 1949.

Embid, Florentino Perez — El Mudejarismo Portugués, Madrid 1944 (2nd edition Madrid, 1955).

Espanca, Túlio — Évora e o seu Distrito, Évora 1959.

Evin, P.A. — L'architecture portugaise au Maroc et le style manuélin, in «Bulletin de l'Institut Français au Portugal» — Lisbonne 1942; Faut-il voir un symbolisme maritime dans la décoration Manuéline ?, in XVI Congrès International d'Histoire de l'Art.

Gonçalves, Flávio — The Architecture and Wood Sculpture of the North of Portugal — 1750-1850 in Portugal and Brazil in transition, ed. by Raymond Sayers and published by Univ. of Minnesota Press, Minneapolis.

Guia de Portugal — Ed. by Biblioteca Nacional de Lisboa, 6 vols. Lisboa 1924.

Gusmão, Artur N. de — A Real Abadia de Alcobaça, Lisboa 1948.

Haupt, A. — Die Baukunst der Renaissance in Portugal, Frankfurt 1850-95.

Inventário Artístico de Portugal — Ed. by Academia Nacional de Belas Artes, Lisbon; 13 vols, published: Portalegre, Coimbra, Santarém, Leiria, Aveiro, Évora.

Kubler, George — Portuguese Plain Architecture, 1972, Wesleyan University Press, Middletown, Conn.

Lambert, Elie — L'église des Templiers de Tomar, XVI Congrès International d'Histoire de l'Art, Rapports et Communications, Vol. II, Lisbonne-Porto 1949.

Lambert — L'Art Manuélin, XVI Congrès International d'Histoire de l'Art, Rapports et Comunications, Vol. II, Lisbonne-Porto 1949.

Lavagnino, Emilio — L'Art Baroque au Portugal, XVI Congrès International d'Histoire de l'Art, Lisbonne, 1949.

Livermore, H. V. — A New History of Portugal, Cambridge Univ. Press, 1966.

Monteiro, Manuel — L'Art Pré-roman au Portugal, in XVI Congrès International d'Histoire de l'Art, Lisbonne 1949.

Murphy — Plans, elevations and views of the church of Batalha — London, 1975.

Portuguese Art, Exhibition of (from 800 to 1800), in Royal Academy of Arts, London 1955 — 56.

Raczynski, Count A. — Les Arts en Portugal, Paris 1847.

Santos, Reynaldo dos — O Estilo Manuelino, Lisboa 1952; O Românico em Portugal, Lisboa 1955; O Azulejo em Portugal, Lisboa 1957.

Simões, J. M. dos Santos — Carreaux Céramiques Hollandais au Portugal et en Espagne, La Haye 1959.

Smith, Robert C. — «Mafra», in «Art Bulletin» (1936); The development of baroque art in Portugal and Brazil, XVI Congrès International d'Histoire de l'Art, Lisbon 1949; The Portuguese Woodcarved Retable, 1600-1750, in «Belas Artes», n. 2, Lisbon 1950; Niccoló Nasoni, Lisbon 1966; The Art of Portugal, 1500-1800, London 1968.

Watson, Walter Crum — Portuguese Architecture, London 1908.